Gematria And Mysticism IN GENESIS

Dr. Akiva Gamliel Belk

- Founder -

B'nai Noach Torah Institute, LLC

http://www.bnti.us

Gematria And Mysticism In Genesis

Copyright © 2012 Dr. Akiva Gamliel Belk

All rights reserved

ISBN – 13: 978-0615701028

ISBN -10: 0615701027

Gematria And Mysticism In Genesis

Publisher

B'nai Noach Torah Institute, LLC,

Post Office Box 14

Cedar Hill, Missouri 63016

First Edition 2012

Gematria And Mysticism In Genesis

DEDICATED

A herder watched after his master's sheep flock.
He was a quiet man exceptionally experienced with stock.

Yet, this bright man could not read or write his name.
A lack of education caused him embarrassment and shame.

He secretly loved a lady he could not wed,
Her father was his master, Kalba Savua whom he dread.

He feared the day his master would learn of his desire
for his beautiful loving daughter Rachel to acquire.

He met this daughter of notability in a pasture as she mourned,
for Rabbi Yochanan a noted Torah Scholar adorned.

Rachel began making informal stops in the pasture land,
to meet him and share words of Torah he would understand.

This herdsman asked deep intriguing questions and debated well,
Rachel loved him and pressed him to study in yeshiva for a spell.

He refused time after time until a drop of water caught his sight.
As the sheep drank he noticed drop after drop of water had might.

He noticed how drops of water cut a hole in hard rock.
He determined that Words of Torah could etch him like the rock.

Gematria And Mysticism In Genesis

He asked Rachel to be his wife,
She said Yes, if he would go to Yeshiva to learn Torah's Life.

He requested to marry Rachel from her father, i.e his boss,
Kalba Savua said no, disowned Rachel and gave them the toss.

Rachel took her things to a shack. She worked long difficult days.
To support her husband whom she sent to learn Torah's Ways.

Thin, cold and hungry Rachel worked on, why? Torah pays.
After years... Israel's Greatest Rabbi would arrive in days.

A huge banquet was made by Kalba Savua who needed advise.
He was sad for disowning Rachel and desired to restore ties.

The Great Rabbi said, I am Akiva, the herdsman. I forgive you!
Kalba Savua said, Move home. I give everything to you!

This book is dedicated to all who lost...
but who will gain eventually...

Gematria And Mysticism In Genesis

Gematria And Mysticism In GENESIS

Table of Contents

DEDICATED..4
FORWARD 9
PREFACE..13
GEMATRIA CHART..19
Genesis Chapter 1..21
   Receiving Pleasure And Enjoying Life........................21
   Genesis Chapter 2..35
   Seven Commands Govern the Entire Universe 35
Genesis Chapter 3..79
   What the Bible Teaches About the Serpent ©...............79
Genesis Chapter 4..113
   What is a Man's Responsibility to His Wife?..............113
Genesis Chapter 5..137
   Adam and Eve Are Equal..137
Genesis Chapter 6..151
   What's In A Name A Word?......................................151
Genesis Chapter 7..167
   God's Might as Seen in the Gematria 617..................167
Genesis Chapter 9..185
Vegetarian Until 1657 From Creation then...................185
Genesis Chapter 10..195
   Speaking Through the Generations 195
Glossary Index..201
Torah References..221
ABOUT THE AUTHOR..223

Gematria And Mysticism In Genesis

Gematria And Mysticism In Genesis

FORWARD

I have known many teachers over the years, some are well known, some are not. One thing I know about the author of this book is that he strives to live what he teaches. Dr. Akiva Gamliel has always required references for any work submitted to him. He follows those rules himself and documents all his work. This book is chocked full of information that most of us have never seen. In this book you will find pearls, nuggets of information, that up until this time have been left to Jewish scholars. For those who understand the many nuances of Hebrew, discovering these hidden treasures is easy. Yet I know it was not like this for Dr. Akiva Gamliel. At the age of 40, like the great Rabbi Akiva, he did not even know the Aleph Bet, i.e. the Hebrew Alphabet. He applied himself through study for many years. He speaks fondly of those days when he learned with 'his teachers' at the Rabbi's table at Yeshiva Toras Chaim during morning breakfast. Since those days Dr. Akiva Gamliel has grown a great deal. He would say, 'It's not enough'. During those years Dr. Akiva Gamliel began studying by invitation. He was invited to learn several evenings a week with a young Rabbi in an old

old trailer in a cow field. Much has changed since then. The young Rabbi at that time was the Director of the Division of Community Services for Yeshiva Toras Chaim Outreach Center. Rabbi, Jacob Meyer is now the head Rabbi of Aish HaTorah, a large Orthodox Congregation and school in Greenwood Village, Colorado.

Back in those early days, Dr. Akiva Gamliel would learn 30 minutes each morning after prayers and before breakfast, with Rabbi David Nussbaum. He is a scholarly Bais Medrash Teacher at Yeshiva Toras Chaim. He is also the son in law of Rosh Ha Yeshiva's Rabbi Isaac Wasserman.

Dr. Akiva Gamliel learned with Rabbi Mordechai Twerski of the Orthodox Congregation Tri Sulom / The Resh Mem Kehilas Beis Yaakov and worked in the Pesach Matzah factory and as a moshgiach.

Dr. Akiva Gamliel also learned with Rabbi Israel Engel of Denver Chabad who is now the Rabbi of Bais Menachem in Denver and also the head of Colorado Chabad.

Dr. Akiva Gamliel's credentials are many. Besides authoring thousands of web pages on the study of the

Torah he also teaches on a weekly basis to hundreds of students through out the world via the internet.

Most of us can use a little help peeling back the layers and uncovering the mysteries of Bereisheit. This book is for anyone who believes that the Torah is like an undiscovered country just waiting to be explored more deeply. As you read and study this book you will find truth if you are truly seeking it So let's begin this journey.

Gematria And Mysticism In Genesis

Gematria And Mysticism In Genesis

PREFACE

The Bible is deep in wisdom, knowledge and is rich in mysteries. Then for every Letter, Word, Phrase, Sentence within the Five Books of the Torah, Genesis, Exodus, Leviticus, Numbers and Deuteronomy there are at least 5,000 possible interpretations. The conundrum within Ha Torah is different than within the rest of the Bible. Within Ha Torah there is a system of Hebrew Letters which each have a numerical value. The numerical values reveal many interesting, perplexing, bewildering and mystifying relationships within the Hebrew Letters, Words, Phrases etc. of Ha Torah that I discuss in this book. Some call this numerology. Others call this Gematria. I call this a study of אות Oht / Sign.

For more than two decades during my daily Torah study I recorded various Signs as they were unveiled to me as well as those revealed to other scholars of much greater stature. As I study Ha Torah The Creator Reveals a glimpse of the hidden. It is a special honor to share from these Gematrias - these Signs in this book. May the Creator be praised!

Hebrew Letters share ties with numbers that unveil many principled secrets if one knows what to look for. An example of this is in Chapter one. Through the Torah one will notice how a Word is spelled. Most Words are consistently spelled the same. However this is not always the situation. When a Word is spelled differently this is a sign one should research around. When a letter is absent or added this is a good place to spend time researching. I call these אותות signs. They are like the entrance to a mine. This is a special place to research because the numerical values have changed. There is a reason.

In this book we are beginning our study chapter by chapter. If God is Willing we intend to continue this through all fifty chapters. I hope you will join in the discussion blog we set up for this book.

Remember, no matter how much information is known about certain Hebrew Word or numbers only a small portion is known in comparison to the entire picture. I have been gathering, compiling and organizing for many years kah nah nah haw raw. Many years can pass between one discovery to another which forms a bridge between two discoveries. Revelations are the product of many bridges. Enclosed in this book are some of these special relationships.

There is a special sweetness in sharing a Torah Gematria / Sign during a wonderful Shabbat or High Holy Day meal.

ACKNOWLEDGEMENTS

My parents have gone on to the next life, may they rest in peace. Momma would have deeply enjoyed the discussion in this book. She was a detail oriented Bible Scholar. We shared many interesting, fiery intense discussions that warm my soul to this day. Momma reminded me more than once, 'Buddy don't give God the hot end of the poker.' Thank you Momma.

Daddy was an orphan from the age of five. He worked fervently to make a place in this world for Momma, my brothers and his grandkids. Life was challenging for him until the very end when he departed in his sleep on Erev Sabbath / Friday night. He would tell associates that he graduated from the school of hard knocks. Daddy's favorite statement was, 'Keep on keeping on.' Thank you Daddy.

My Former Father – In – law, may he rest in peace, used to say, 'Don't give me roses when I'm dead. Give me roses while I'm alive [when I can enjoy them.] His favorite statement was about tithing. He would tell his congregants, You don't pick your groceries up at this store then walk across the street and pay for them at another store.'

I acknowledge that my Step – Mother – In – Law is truly a kind Spiritual Lady. I am blessed thank God! Kah Nah Naw Haw Raw. Katie listens to every concern with patience and then offers encouragement and prayer. She cares about other people. She is a most excellent example for others to follow. May she be blessed with good health and a long life... Thank you Katie.

The greatest acknowledgement that one can make is to say and to mean the Lord God is my Creator. He is King of this Universe and of all that exists. He is Holy and His Name is Holy. God Willing someday in the future I will join the many individuals already in the heavens with our Creator and express my many appreciations to them. In this book I share a few stories about them.

My acknowledgement to my wife is that a praiseworthy wife is so rare. It is very difficult to reach such a lofty level. Thank you for trying, Dad Belk said, "trying counts!' He was right. Please be understanding regarding those rare occasions when you may not have reached the highest level of Aishet Chayil. After all look who you are married to. I made it a challenge even though many times it was not intentional. Thank you for trying!!

My acknowledgement to my brothers is to seek the truth that you do not know and when you find it do not be afraid to embrace it. King Solomon said that the Torah [Law] of the Lord is perfect. Why would God want to replace the Torah?

A very important acknowledgement is to my two sons and two step sons. REGARDLESS of what anyone tells you, each of you are required to honor your mother and your father every hour of your life. I wish that I had been a much better example for you to observe and follow. Never cease to teach your children to *Honor their father and their mother so that their days may be long upon the land which the Lord our God Gives them... [regardless of their age]*, Shemot / Exodus 20.12.

Someday my grandchildren will read this book when they are older and curious and want to know more about their Zadie. To them I acknowledge that אמת Emet / Truth will stand on its own. Look at the Letters. Every letter of Truth stands on it own. Each Letter of Truth has two legs and a foundation. Truth will stand up to all questions. Never be afraid to ask many questions. The opposite of Emet is a שקר sheker, a lie. Look at the

Letters. Each letter of a sheker has no foundation and only one leg to stand on. Our Sages Teach a sheker will fall before Emet..

Gematria And Mysticism In Genesis

GEMATRIA CHART

Aleph	א	1			
Bet	ב	2			
Gimmel	ג	3			
Dalet	ד	4			
Hey	ה	5			
Vav	ו	6			
Zayin	ז	7			
Chet	ח	8			
Tet	ט	9			
Yud	י	10			
Chof	כ	20	Final	ך	500
Lamid	ל	30			
Mem	מ	40	Final	ם	600
Nun	נ	50	Final	ן	700
Samech	ס	60			
Ayin	ע	70			
Pey	פ	80	Final	ף	800
Tzzadi	צ	90		ץ	900
Quf	ק	100			
Reish	ר	200			
Shin	ש	300			
Tav	ת	400			

Gematria And Mysticism In Genesis

Genesis Chapter 1
Receiving Pleasure And Enjoying Life

In 5760 I wrote, *Our world can at times be a most trying place. Then there are other times that our world is the center of wonderful experiences and everything that's good. Sometimes we live in the world that is lonely, cold and desolate. Then there are other times when we shift to the happier side of life. The path from good to bad and back to good, from elation to depression and back to elation, from crowds to lonely isolations and back to crowds is like the shifting sands of the ocean...*

Gematria And Mysticism In Genesis

Dear Ones, there is a tranquil place in life that is not centered on what one has or doesn't have. That place is studying and learning The Torah.

What places The Torah on such a high level? What makes the Bible Holy? What is Biblical Holiness?

The Word קָדֵשׁ Kodesh means Holy. Dictionaries define Holy as being saintly, godly, pious, religious, devout, or God-fearing, etc. However these descriptions are a bit distant from what Holiness really is. Misunderstanding the meaning of Holiness will cause one to misunderstand the Bible.

I like J.D. Strong's definition. In his concordance, i.e. Strong's Concordance he defines קָדֵשׁ / as apartness, as Holiness as separateness. Dr. Strong is correct in stating that Holiness is 'Separateness.' Think of it like this. The land of Israel is the Holy Land. Why? Israel is 'separated' from the rest of the world. Jerusalem is the Holy City. Jerusalem is separated from all other cities in Israel. The Western Wall is part of the Holy Temple. The Holy Temple is separated from the city of Jerusalem. Within the Holy Temple there was the Holy Holy Place. The Holy Holy Place was separated from the Holy Temple, which was separated from the Holy City, Jerusalem, which was separated from the Holy Land Israel, which was separated from all other land in the world. In a similar way The Torah is part of the Bible but The Torah is separated from the other parts of the Bible.

Dear Ones why do people of many faiths travel to the Holy Land... to the Holy City... to the Western Wall...? It's not by chance. Discovering the answer to this question should bring us into that place where we can be tranquil and enjoy the best of what life has to offer. Then God Willing, from this place we can enjoy the good things in life. The Gematria of the Word קָדְשׁ Kodesh is 404. The Word דָת Dawt meaning Law, Order or Royal Decree expresses the Desire of The Lord God for each of us as written in the Torah. In other words The Lord God is saying to the Children of Israel, I want you to observe Holiness. The, the Lord God is saying to each of us, observe holiness. So mystically we see the desire of the Lord God revealed in the Torah for each of us.

קָדְשׁ
Kodesh
404 = 300שׁ 4ד 100ק

Gematria And Mysticism In Genesis

דָּת
Dawt
404 = 400ת 4ד

We see the matching Gematrias. Now Observe how knowledge that is not normally accessible to us, opens up its petals, like a flower of possibility in two additional Gematrias. In Leviticus 10.1-3 the Letter Aleph, which Represents God, is added to the Word קֹדֶשׁ Kodesh meaning separated. This also is noted in Exodus 29.44. The Aleph is added to Kodesh twice in the entire Torah. The Letter Aleph, at the front of Kodesh, is normally not how Kodesh is spelled. With the Letter Aleph added This means, 'I will be Sanctified' or 'I will be Separated'. The Letter Aleph changes the Gematria from 404 to 405. So far we don't see the picture. The picture is just beginning to develop. In a few pages it will be clear. We must inquire, why did our Creator add the Letter Aleph? Always take note of spelling changes. Now we must explore some. All the sudden lights go on when we discover the combined Gematria of four Words. The four Words are *the sons of Aaron, Nadab and Abihu...*' The Gematria of these four Words combined is also 405. This reveals to us that Nadab and Abihu did not Sanctify The Lord God. They added Alien fire. This tells us that our Creator's Holiness can NEVER be compromised even one small degree.

Gematria And Mysticism In Genesis

וַיִּקְחוּ בְנֵי־אַהֲרֹן נָדָב וַאֲבִיהוּא אִישׁ
מַחְתָּתוֹ וַיִּתְּנוּ בָהֵן אֵשׁ וַיָּשִׂימוּ עָלֶיהָ
קְטֹרֶת וַיַּקְרִיבוּ לִפְנֵי יְהוָה אֵשׁ זָרָה
אֲשֶׁר לֹא צִוָּה אֹתָם :

וַתֵּצֵא אֵשׁ מִלִּפְנֵי יְהוָה וַתֹּאכַל אוֹתָם
וַיָּמֻתוּ לִפְנֵי יְהוָה :

Leviticus 10.1, 2
And they took, **the sons of Aaron, Nadab and Abihu,** *took each his censer, and put fire in it, and put incense on it, and offered alien fire before the Lord, which He Commanded them not. And there went out fire from the Lord, and devoured them, and they died before the Lord.*

וַיֹּאמֶר מֹשֶׁה אֶל־אַהֲרֹן הוּא אֲשֶׁר־דִּבֶּר
יְהוָה ׀ לֵאמֹר בִּקְרֹבַי **אֶקָּדֵשׁ** וְעַל־פְּנֵי
כָל־הָעָם אֶכָּבֵד וַיִּדֹּם אַהֲרֹן :

And he, Moses said to Aaron, *'It is that Word The Lord Spoke, saying through those near Me* **I shall**

be sanctified *and on the face of all the people I will be Glorified'* and Aaron was silent.

אֱקָדֵשׁ
Kodesh
405 = 300ש 4ד 100ק 1א

בְּנֵי־אַהֲרֹן נָדָב וַאֲבִיהוּא
The sons of Aaron, Nadab and Abihu...

405 = 1א 6ו 5ה 10י 2ב 1א 6ו   2ב 4ד 50נ   50ן 200ר 5ה 1א   10י 50נ 2ב

Now, through this Gematria we get a serious peak into the degree of Holiness that is required even though we may not be able to understand that level of holiness. In Judaism we teach there are fifty levels one strives to reach throughout their life time. The highest level is perfection. Mystically we note that Nadab and Abihu may have come very close to this level. In fact they may have actually reached this level. Reaching the fiftieth level is a great great accomplishment for a human. However, living on the fiftieth level is an entirely different challenge.

Now the issue is that there is a fine balance in what our Creator desires. Now lets consider our

Creator's Creating.

From God's six days of Creating we gain a perspective on enjoying the good things in life. In Genesis 1:4 we observe that the Creator of the universe receives special pleasure from the Light He Revealed. Let's stop and focus on how light gives us such pleasure for a minute.

We at B'nai Noah Torah Institute, LLC teach that the utmost enjoyment in life is the pleasure we receive from the Revelation of God {Enlightenment}. We arrive at this conclusion from studying Genesis 1.4.

First, the word אור "light" is spelled Aleph (1) on the right, Vav (6) in the middle and Reish (200) on the left. The three holy Letters equal 207.

Now let's observe them in their proper order from right to left:

אור
200 = Reish - 6 = Vav - 1 = Aleph

"Ohr" was created as a directional word from right to left. This means that the Letters travel from the right where God is to the left. As they travel they increase in their numerical value. In the word "Ohr" this is especially significant because the Letter on the right is an Aleph. The Aleph represents the One and only God, Creator of everything. From the Letter Aleph we learn that Ohr emanates from God flooding all Creation with His Revelation. The Ohr that Creation experienced on Day One was that of the Lord. It was not sun, moon or starlight. It was not a created light since this light was always in existence. It was אֶת־הָאוֹר *The Revealed Light*. God chose to Reveal some of Himself, in His eternal existence. He revealed the light of The Torah. He unwrapped a revelation of His Will to us!

How do we know this? Gematria supports these statements fully. The Gematria of the Letters Eht Ha Ohr equal 613. I discuss this in a greater extent in chapter 1 of my book <u>Mysterious Signs of Gematria and Mysticism In Genesis</u> so we will briefly discuss the significance of 613 here. The number 613 is the exact number of Commands given to the Children of Israel in The Torah.

It is most significant that Eht Ha Ohr occurs in the center of the Verse, *"God saw that 'The Light' was good.*" This teaches us that the center of everything is what God has Revealed to each of us in the 613 Commands of The Torah.

Now I understand that this ancient Teaching is very new to some of us. Yet, just think about this for a little while. Let it soak in some. Our Creator expresses what He Desires for us. We are to honor Him through the Observance of 613 Commands. Some of these Commands are for B'nai Noah, i.e the children who are descendants of Noah and his wife Na'amah. Some commands are for just men. Some Commands are just for women. Some Commands are for the Priests. Some Commands are just for the High Priest. God Willing in another book I will list and explain some of the Commands. However for right now our concern is to begin realizing that the center of a tranquil place is learning and Observing the 613 Commands. Most of us do this already with a few exceptions. The exceptions are the areas of our life that we have not yielded to God.

The point is that the 613 of The Torah Commands are at the center of all good... and where the greatest pleasure of life exists. Right now this is just a statement. However as we learn together we will discover this more and more. We start to arrive in the place of tranquility when we accept the 613 Torah Commands are at the center of all good. We will learn the Commands that pertain to each of us. We return to the Word אור which offers another view of light. Ohr is the Gematria of 207 which relates to זְקֵנִים Ze Kay Neem which is another form of light. זְקֵנִים / Ze Kay Neem is the light emanating from the wise, and from the elders. So we have the Ohr emanating from God the Creator and we have the Ohr that emanates from the meaning of elders, the wise. There are many pictures of a grandparent teaching a grandchild something special that may come to mind. How about a grandfather teaching his grandchild to catch a fish or a grandmother teaching a grand daughter to bake Challah.

207 = 1א 6ו 200ר

207 = 7ז 100ק 50נ 10י 40ם

The point here is the input by which an elder enriches our life is a special blessing from our Creator.

Gematria And Mysticism In Genesis

King David Wrote:
Tehillim / Psalms 19.8 [KJV 19.7]
תּוֹרַת יְהֹוָה תְּמִימָה מְשִׁיבַת נָפֶשׁ עֵדוּת יְהֹוָה נֶאֱמָנָה מַחְכִּימַת פֶּתִי׃

The Torah of the Lord is perfect restoring the soul, the testimony of the Lord is sure, making wise the simple.

The Perfect Torah has the power to restore.
There are three points of great importance here.
First, ONLY The Torah, i.e. Genesis, Exodus, Leviticus, Numbers and Deuteronomy, are Perfect.

Second, Only The Torah of the Lord can return and restore the soul of each of us...

Third, Only The Torah of the Lord can make those who are foolish wise.

In other words Observing that The Torah has the power to improve ones ethics and morals even to the place of תָּמִים Taw Meem meaning Perfect / Blameless. All religious teachings of any value are based upon the position that an individual needs to improve and needs help in their desire to improve. Observing that The Torah is the help one needs. Dear Ones how can one reach the place of tranquility if they have no way to improve?

It is necessary for us to lay this foundation early on in our discussion. Observing The Torah will bring tranquility into our lives. This is not about one religion verses another. This is not about the new Testament verses the Old Testament. This is about the pure Truth of God's Word being understood!! Just think a little about what is being offered here.

Honoring ones parents brings tranquility into ones life. This is a Command of The Torah that reverberates throughout the Bible.

Do you think it is OK to curse God? Do you think it is OK to damn God? Do you think it is OK to steal? Do you think it is OK to lie? Each of these are Commands based in the perfect Torah that reverberate throughout the Bible. When we Observe these Commands we are on the road to a more tranquil life. I am saying that the teachings in the Bible are founded within the 613 Commands written in the Perfect Torah! We need to learn to Observe the Command our Creator requires of us. If we desire to enjoy life to the fullest.

Gematria And Mysticism In Genesis

Genesis Chapter 2
Seven Commands Govern the Entire Universe

The second that Adam and Eve were Created laws existed that guided all behavior in the universe. All creation is governed by these laws. We call these Laws the Seven Commands. We are obligated to observe the Seven Commandments. They are regarded as the foundations of all human and moral progress. All creation may attain spiritual perfection, by the observance of these laws and obtain a good life in the life hereafter.

Gematria And Mysticism In Genesis

Dear Ones, does anyone think this world can govern itself? I know there are evolutionists that still believe and argue the development and diversification of one form of life to another during the history of the earth. They can argue all they desire yet science has discovered plant life has separate DNA from human DNA. If evolution were correct the news papers would blast that humankind has been traced back to the original single cell. That has not happened! In fact the opposite has happened.

The point is that all earth is complicated. Even the single blade of grass is complicated. These many complications point to a Creator. DNA will eventually prove the Creation Account in The Torah to be 100 percent accurate. Before we move on I would like to say that it is possible that each day of creation is a period in time that could be millions of years. This would explain the age difference in what some scientists call ape like humans that appear to be millions of years old. Dear Ones they could be. Remember the Angels were created in day two or period two of creation. Angels could be millions of human years old having been created before humankind.

Gematria And Mysticism In Genesis

Remember two angels came to earth and became corrupt? They had relationships with the daughters of man. It would be interesting to examine the DNA of the ancient remains scientists discovered. The remains could reveal a most interesting story.

However our point here is that we have a Creator and that DNA points much more towards being crafted than an uneducated cell developing its self.

There are mysterious powers within the Letters of The Torah. As we research with computers we discover more. In the past thirty years Bible Codes were discovered. More are being discovered. They reveal the great depth to which The Torah was written. No writer of any time has written in Moses's depth. We know Moses was a scribe. We know Moses wrote what the Creator Instructed him to write. We understand that The Torah of the Lord is a very unique Book of the Greatest Holiness and Mysticism! The point to this is that our Creator who went to such great detail in the development of all forms of life and the DNA for these forms of life would not develop humankind and place them here on earth without a plan to follow. Our Creator Instructed Adam and Eve in the Seven Commands he desired them to Observe.

Gematria And Mysticism In Genesis

The Seven Commands are:

Commandment One:
Establish and Follow A System of Rulership / Justice

Commandment Two:
Do Not Blaspheme God's Holy Name

Commandment Three:
Only Worship the Creator. Idolatry Is Prohibited.

Commandment Four:
Do Not Murder! Do Not Shed blood!

Commandment Five:
Do Not Take Another Man's Wife! Do Not Commit Adultery!

Commandment Six:
Do Not Steal!

Commandment Seven:
Be Kind To Animals!

The Seven Commands are founded in Genesis 2.16 and 17.

וַיְצַו יְהוָה אֱלֹהִים עַל־הָאָדָם
לֵאמֹר מִכֹּל עֵץ־הַגָּן אָכֹל תֹּאכֵל:

וַיְצַו

Vah Yih Tzahv
And He [the Lord God] Commanded
112 = 6ו 90צ 10י 6ו

בַּעֲלֵי

Bah Ah Lay
Possessor / Owner
112 = 10י 30ל 70ע 2ב

We should be able to see the relationship of the Lord God who Commanded Ha Adam, meaning the man with that of being the Possessor and the Owner of all...

Genesis 2.16 is the first place in The Torah where the Word וַיְצַו Vah Yih Tzahv And He [the Lord God] Commanded. As a result we stop to examine what God Commanded. Then we follow a logical process we see what our Creator Intended.

There is One Who Commands and there are those who receive His Commands. The One Who Commands is the Creator who is Higher. The Creator is in Charge. The Creator is above all of us who are Commanded. So when The Torah Says, 'He Commanded'. We are to understand this plus the structure that comes with it. The Commands are not necessarily listed in chronological order.

Commandment One:

Establish and Follow A System of Rulership / Justice

First, God is the Creator of everything. As Creator of everything God is Superior to what He Created. God is Superior to man, all creatures, the universe... everything. God is Possessor and Owner of all. We understand this.

Now man is introduced to God in Genesis 1.28 with the words *God Said... to them*. Then a second time in Genesis 1.29 again with the words *God Said...* Then in Genesis 2.16 we read, *'the Lord God Commanded the man...'* So far it is clear to us that up until this point The Torah only records *'God Said'* to the man... This is the first time the Lord God Commanded the man. There is a very big difference between *'God Said'* and *'the Lord God Commanded!'* The word Commanded in Genesis 2.16 is from the same root as Commandments, as in the Ten Commandments in Exodus 20. The meaning for the word

'Commanded' is 'Law'. The meaning of 'Commandments' is 'LAWS'. This deviation in Genesis from *'God Said..'* to 'the Lord God Commanded..' is the beginning of required observances... social laws... commandments. So God as the Judge of the universe, that He Created, now Sits in judgment over the man and his wife. The man as we shall demonstrate now sits in judgment over all mankind and over all the creatures of the earth.

In English translations of the Bible one could easily pass by the word COMMANDED thousands of times not noticing that this is the place in The Torah where social laws for all mankind began. One could even delve into non Jewish Hebrew concordances or lexicons and still miss what is actually happening here.

When the Lord God Commands the man, *'You may certainly eat from every tree in the Garden. But from the Tree of Knowledge of what is good and evil, you shall not eat from it...'* the Lord God Established social laws! One may ask, How Did

God Establish social laws beginning here?

The Lord God could have Said, 'Do not eat from the Tree of Knowledge.' Then if the man or his wife had eaten from it they would be guilty of just disobedience. However, because of the way in which the Lord God Worded His Commandments He Established two categories:

First, What belongs to you {the man} and his wife is acceptable to eat.

Second, What does not belong to Adam or to Eve, is not acceptable to eat.

By doing this the Lord God Establishes a series of laws that He as Ruler of the universe Governs over. If one or more of these Commands that He Established are disobeyed, then He as Judge Passes Judgment on the disobedient.

Next we see the Lord God Establishing the man as ruler over His {the Lord God's} Creation by Bringing every creature He Created to the man to see 'what he {the man} would call them,' {Genesis 2.19}. The word יִקְרָא 'To Call' {Yek Raw} means 'to call' or 'to summon' each creature. Yek Raw does NOT MEAN TO NAME. So whatever CALL the man used to summon each creature to him became the creature's name by proclamation of the Lord God. This could be considered like a dog whistle that beckons one's dog to come. The sound the whistle makes calls the dog but the sound or the call is not actually the dog's name. IT IS IMPORTANT TO UNDERSTAND THIS!

So we now see a chain of commands developing. The man was inferior to his Creator, the Lord God, but superior to the creatures the Lord God had Given the man Authority to summon. This is the establishment of a system of rulership and justice. From this we can understand that just as the man had authority to summon any creature, the Lord God Had Authority to Summon the man. We know this because the Lord God Vah Yek Raw, Called, 'Summoned' the man, {Genesis 3.9} and the man responded. That teaches us that the Lord God Has a Name whereby He is Called, man has a name whereby he is called and each creature of Creation has a name whereby they are called. Now man could summon each creature but the Lord God Could Summon each creature and the man. From this we learn the honor placed upon each level of rulership. This establishes a system of governing before other humans existed.

יְהוָה the Lord = {Prohibition against blasphemy} Dovid Ha Melech said, *'And they shall praise everything from Aleph To Tav of the Name of the Lord for His Name alone is Exalted.'* Psalms 148:13 The presence of the Lord's Name in written form, in spoken form or in thought form is to be exalted. Any awareness of His Name is to be exalted!! This is necessary because of the Very Holy Essence of His Name. the Lord's Name is unlike any other name. The Torah says,

וְלֹא יְחַלְּלוּ אֶת־שֵׁם קָדְשִׁי
'And you shall not profane, make common anything from Aleph to Tav of My Holy Name...' Leviticus 22.32

Gematria And Mysticism In Genesis

Gematria And Mysticism In Genesis

Commandment Two:

Do Not Blaspheme God's Holy Name

יְהוָה

the Lord
26 =

הֵיטֵב

Hay Tayv
To to good to do well diligently
26 = 2ב 9ט 10י 5ה

Again it should be obvious if one does good, if one does well, that one is honoring our Creator. What does the Psalmist say? Depart from Evil, and do good; seek peace, and pursue it, Psalms 34.14. the emphasis is upon doing good. The emphasis is not on blaspheming the Creator's name. This is about our actions. Our actions should praise, and bless, and honor our Creator. This Command is more about what we should rather than what we should not be doing.

Each creature paid homage to God as Ruler and Creator of the universe and to the man as ruler of the earth by the authority of the Lord God. The man paid homage to the Lord God only. Notice that the name the creatures of the earth paid homage to was 'God', representing only the attribute of Justice. Notice the name the man paid homage to was 'the Lord God,' representing both the attributes of Justice and Grace. This is very important!

Many non Jews normally think of the name God as God but creatures in Creation knew the meaning of God to be 'Ruler / Judge.' The man knew the Lord God as 'Merciful Ruler / Judge.' This only occurs when the plural Name God meaning Ruler / Judge is combined with the Singular Name the Lord meaning Merciful. That teaches us that God is actually Singular and NOT plural. Understanding the full intention and meaning of God shown ORIGINALLY at Creation to all Creation is extremely important.

Unfortunately it seems as though the intention and

meaning of God has been displaced by some with FALSE DOCTRINE heading into the twenty-first century. It is imperative that we, as the elements of Creation return to the original understanding of God, that being the Lord God, the Merciful Ruler / Judge.

It is from this understanding that we intuitively know, just like a new born knows without instruction how to suckle their mother's breast, that we are to honor God and to honor His Holy Name the Lord God! In other words, honoring God and His Holy Name is a natural instinct established from Creation. It is a physical law in the same sense that birds, fish and animals mate after their own kind... that plant life does not naturally mix. Wheat produces wheat. Apple trees produce apples, which produce apple seeds, which produces apple trees. It is a series of natural relationships of the sun, moon and stars to earth's rotation... In the same way, we understand that we are to honor the Lord God and His Name as the Merciful Ruler / Judge.

Life before the flood was considerably different

than it is today. Creatures did not feed on each other. All creatures lived in TOTAL PEACE. Man was 100% vegetarian. The world then had a harmony. The sun was never too bright or too hot. Rain and snow did not exist. Mountains and oceans like we now have did not exist. Storms of any kind were unheard of. Man did not cover the entire earth as we know it today. The world then was a very special and wonderful place. Everyone spoke the same language before the flood. God's Presence was felt everywhere. God Was understood in a special way by His Creation everywhere.

All residents of earth could travel to the entrance of Garden of Eden. They could see the angel with the flaming sword in person. Man had a closeness then that man does not have today. Man still had direct connections to Garden of Eden that were visually evident for anyone to see. For over nine hundred years the residents of earth could speak with the original man. They learned first hand about the Seven Commands if they chose. Man then had direct connections that do not exist today.

Gematria And Mysticism In Genesis

In the first world, man's responsibility of honoring the Lord God was clearly understood by all residents of earth. Man then understood that He was to worship only the Lord God. Clearly both Cain and Abel understood the requirement to honor the Lord God. We who did not live in that day think we understand but often do not. We will discuss this in Chapter Four. They both brought offerings... It is also clear that Noah and his sons understood the requirement to honor the Lord God. Noah brought offerings to the Lord God. We will discuss Cain's offering later.

אֱלֹהִים God = {Prohibition against idolatry} Anytime we read the word God as we do here we are reminded that this Name is in reference to God our Creator and Judge. We are also reminded that when the exact same word is used with a small e for elohim it is in reference to gods with a small g. Understanding what this means is not complicated. The Torah says, *You must not have other gods before My Essence.* Exodus 20.3 So when The Torah uses the Name God as it does here we are reminded to be careful not to serve other gods. We are reminded of the prohibition of idolatry.

Gematria And Mysticism In Genesis

Gematria And Mysticism In Genesis

Commandment Three:

Only Worship the Creator.
Idolatry Is Prohibited.

אֱלֹהִים
God
= 86

עַבְדֵי
Servants of
86 = 10י 4ד 2ב 70ע

The sons of Israel said to Joseph (in Genesis 50.17), we are servants of the God of your father. They were saying that they bow down only to God. There is no other God in there lives. They Worshiped only the God of Joseph's father. The Gematria relationship is for us to understand that as servants of God we are to worship only Him as God. This means idolatry is prohibited!!

The Lord God Who Created everything is to be honored with our worship and praise as God, who Rules / Judges with Righteous Judgment. Idolatry

53

is worshiping His Creation like: the stars, the moon, the sun, plants and animals. Idolatry of any form opposes honor to the Creator. In fact it is rebellion against the Creator of the Universe.

The world before the flood had a special relationship with the Lord God that is not the same as now. Today we have hundreds of thousands of laws that did not exist then. Why are all these laws necessary today but were not necessary then?

It has to do with how man lived in relationship with the Lord God. Man's sense of understanding God's Will was very keen then. As man moved further and further away from God, eventually He was destroyed. Idolatry was destroyed! Then a new sense of awareness was reestablished after the flood that was established with Noah and his sons. That special sense of understanding the Lord God was reestablished again with the Seven Noach Commandments They demonstrated their sense of understanding through sacrifice to the Lord God immediately after the flood. Everyone was present! Noah as the family head was also the High Priest.

Gematria And Mysticism In Genesis

He offered sacrifices and worship to the Lord God.

The residents of the world originally understood that one simple word, God, God meant all creation was to honor their Creator by not worshiping anyone or anything else.

עַל־הָאָדָם to the Adam = {Prohibition against bloodshed} Here the words Ahl {on, upon, over, against} represent the prohibition of bloodshed. When the Creator Appoints us to be over 'the man' it has the impact of protecting or guarding the man. On the other hand the last two letters of Adam represent dom {blood} so one could say the Creator prohibits the shedding of blood דם. We will discuss this more in Chapter four.

Gematria And Mysticism In Genesis

Commandment Four:

Do Not Murder!
Do Not Shed blood!

עַל־הָאָדָם

Ayl Haw Aw Dawm
To the man (meaning man and woman here)
150 = 40 מ 4 ד 5 א 5 ה   30 ל 70 ע

יִכָּנַע

Yee Caw Nah
To Be humble
150 = 70 ע 50 נ 20 כ 10 י

Please notice the progression of the Letters from right to left of the word יִכָּנַע Yee Caw Nah. The first Letter is 10 then 20 then 50 and finally 70. When one is not humble, when one is angry, they, so to speak, go from 10 to 20 to 50 to 70... No one wants to be around when they get to seventy. When we study the emanations of God we learn that on the right is Kindness and on the Left is

Strength. We are constructed in God's Spiritual Image. When our anger raises up it charges towards strength on the left rather than Kindness on the right. אף / Ahf meaning anger is one on the right and 80 on the left.

When we are Commanded '*To the Man*' or '*For the man*' we are reminded that just as we have this great ability to love and honor God we have the power and the strength to do the opposite. Yet the difference between man and animals is, we have a choice. Animals have instinct. For the man to be made in the Spiritual Image of our Creator we have to possess the Strength to get angry and the strength to do awful things because of anger, Kaw Naw Nah Haw Raw! Yet we do not have to do these things. Thank God! We only need to possess the strength to do them. So what we need to do is the opposite of anger. We need to יָכְנַע Yee Caw Nah to be humble!! When we consider the word anger with a Gematria of 81 we need to go from Strength 80 on the left to Kindness 1 on the right. Remember that the Letter Aleph on the right represents God!!

In Genesis 9.6 The Torah states, *'Who so sheds man's blood, by man shall his blood be shed.'* It is a general law, applicable to all, having been given in the pre-Abrahamic era; 'his blood shall be shed' refers to the sword, the only form of death where blood is shed.

The prohibition of shedding blood extends back to the Command, 'You may certainly eat from every tree in the Garden,' which also meant eating animals was prohibited. It is also clear from Creation that all creatures and man were to feed on plant life {Genesis 1. 29,30}. Before the flood, plant life was considerably different than in today's world. The climate, the soil and other conditions were perfect. The product of the field was considerably superior to ours proceeding the flood.

Man understood that taking the life of any creature was prohibited. This was clearly demonstrated by the man and his mate sewing fig leaves together as opposed to taking the life of an animal {Genesis 3.7}. The Lord God had not Given the man authority to take life. The man intuitively understood that life was precious.

We also have the example of Kayin {Cain} and Hevel {Abel}. Cain murdered his brother, Abel. Yet in Cain's disobedience, the Lord had Compassion. From this unfortunate murder in the first family we learn of the prohibition of murder in accordance with Genesis 9:6. the Lord Said, *'Therefore, whoever kills {not murders} Cain, revenge will be taken on him {Cain} sevenfold.'* Meaning do not kill Cain. Vengeance will be taken on him by his descendant Lemech in the seventh generation....

The point is that earth's inhabitants would have, in the normal course of justice which was established by the Lord God, taken Cain before the man, {Adam} the ruler, the high priest and judge of earth to be judged. The man would have found Cain, his own son, guilty and sentenced him to die by the sword. Justice would have been served. However the Lord had compassion on the man because Cain at that time was the man and the woman's only son. Justice would have to wait until after Seth was born.

Yet we learn from this verse that mankind had already been instructed in revenging murder. The Lord's Attribute of Mercy Intervened... Notice only the Attribute of Mercy {the Lord} is present in dealing with Cain. Please notice that from Genesis 4.1 through Genesis 4.16 the Name the Lord occurs eight times. The word God occurs only once in Genesis Four. The one occurrence of God in Genesis Four is in relation to His Justice. The son that was taken {Hevel} was restored {Seth}! It is at the birth of Seth whose Neshamah {soul} was that of Hevel, Eve said *'God has granted me another offspring in place of Hevel.'* The soul in Seth was the Neshamah of Hevel. We call this transmigration of the soul.

לֵאמֹר Saying = {Prohibition against adultery} This represents the proper sequence of events. A father and mother of the same beliefs and observances have the responsibility of passing on to their children utterances, sayings and words of The Torah. So when The Torah says Lay Mohr it is in reference to the necessary sequence of proper events required to pass on an utterance of The Torah. In other words one must get married to an individual of the same belief with the same goals and ideals. They must have children. They must raise their children in Observance of The Torah. When these conditions exist, then, and only then, is it possible to pass on utterances of The Torah.

Gematria And Mysticism In Genesis

Commandment Five:

Do Not Take Another Man's Wife!
Do Not commit Adultery!

לֵאמֹר
Saying
271 = 200ר 40מ 1א 30ל

יֵאָסֵר
Yay Aw Sayr
To Be Bound
271 = 200ר 40מ 1א 30ל

Teachings... Sayings are supposed to come with bindings with ties. The Teachings here are from the Torah. The bindings are to the Teachings of the Torah. Among the Orthodox the rate of divorce is very low. The reason is in most instances the grand parents are bound to the Torah Teachings. The Parents are bound to the Torah Teachings. The husband and wife are bound to the Torah Teachings. Being bound to the teachings is being committed to the Teachings... We understand!

Originally, after the woman was taken from the man's side, she was called or summoned to the man as the 'woman'. After the man's sin he then changed the call or summon from the 'woman' to 'Chavah' {Eve}.

Before the man's sin he made a proclamation as ruler over all the earth as follows: 'Therefore a man shall leave his father and mother and cling to his wife and they shall be one flesh.' Genesis 2.24

How did the man know about the concept of 'Father' or 'Mother?' What did he know about leaving father or mother? The man had neither. This shows us that the Lord God Had Instructed the man in the sanctity of marriage, the birth and raising of children, and the family. It is clear from this statement that the Lord God Taught the man that he and his wife were 'one flesh'. So the terms husband and wife were established from the beginning to be 'one flesh'.

From these we learn that man and man or woman and woman do not equal 'one flesh.' We learn that man and beast or woman and beast do not equal 'one flesh.' We learn that God, the Creator Who is a Spirit NOT FLESH and woman do not equal 'one flesh'. From the beginning the term 'one flesh' has only meant the union by marriage of one husband {singular} and one wife {singular}. From the beginning God Blessed the relationship of the only human male and female. God Said to them {instructed them}, *'Be fruitful and multiply'*. This meant, together only, were they *'one flesh'*. This same command of 'Be fruitful and multiply' was also given twice to Noah and his sons after the flood. Noah had his wife, Shem had his wife, Ham had his wife, Yafes had his wife They were four married couples. This has always been God's plan.

Now we must notice that on three separate occasions {Genesis 1:28 before the fall, and Genesis 9:1 and Genesis 9:7 after the flood} the blessing, 'Be fruitful and multiply,' was spoken only by God, representing the Attribute of Justice. This demonstrates to mankind the sanctity of

marriage. Marriage was created to be Echad, 'ONE', just as God is 'ONE.' Marriage is between a man and a woman. Homosexuality is a serious sin. Many Homosexual's say they would rather be straight. Some say that they were born with these urges. That is possible. Yet if an individual does not control their urges of homosexuality and acts on them that is a sin. Homosexuality is immoral!
Yet our purpose is not to beat up on Homosexuals. It is to say the Creators plan is for men and women to have children and loving families.

The act of taking a wife is established in The Torah and in the Talmud as וַיִּקַּח Vah Yee Kah Ach, meaning 'and he took'. וַיִּקַּח is a very male dominating word that could be easily misunderstood. One has to wonder why The Torah uses such a male dominating powerful word / for marriage. וַיִּקַּח is a forceful Word. The first and second usage of וַיִּקַּח will assist us understanding the intent and usage.

The Word אִישׁ Eesh meaning man is the ninth word in verse 12. The first usage of אִישׁ Eesh is found in Genesis 2.24.

It is important to note that prior to this usage of אִישׁ Eesh the word used for man / woman was הָאָדָם Ha Adam. The Torah States that the Lord Took from the Adam [representing both Adam and Eve] a wife / a woman.

וַיִּבֶן יְהוָה אֱלֹהִים ׀ אֶת־הַצֵּלָע אֲשֶׁר־לָקַח מִן־הָאָדָם לְאִשָּׁה וַיְבִאֶהָ אֶל־הָאָדָם :

Genesis 2.22
And He, the Lord God Built everything from Aleph to Tav of <u>the side</u> that He Took from Ha Adam into a wife and He Came with her to Ha Adam.

What is very notable here is the Word לָקַח Law Kah Ach meaning '*to take*'. This is the very Word that The Torah uses to describe Abraham in marriage to Keturah in Genesis 25. 1.

Genesis 25.1

Gematria And Mysticism In Genesis

וַיֹּסֶף אַבְרָהָם וַיִּקַּח אִשָּׁה וּשְׁמָהּ קְטוּרָה׃

And Again He Avraham and took a wife and her name was Keturah.

Notice the combination of how the words are used:

Genesis 2.22

אֲשֶׁר־לָקַח מִן־הָאָדָם לְאִשָּׁה

...that He Took from Ha Adam into a wife...

Genesis 25.1

אַבְרָהָם וַיִּקַּח אִשָּׁה וּשְׁמָהּ קְטוּרָה

Avraham and took a wife and her name was Keturah.

In both instances the word לָקַח Law Kah Ach meaning 'to take' and וַיִּקַּח Vah Yee Kah Ach meaning 'and he took' each have to do with taking a wife. Why is this important? It is important because the first time the word אִשָּׁה meaning 'wife / woman' is used in The Torah is immediately after Eve was taken from Ha Adam which represented both of them. This is the term the Lord used to describe a wife / a woman. Then after this Adam Says, '…she was taken from אִישׁ Eesh. The soul of the man and the woman are one soul in two bodies. When a man and woman come together it is supposed to be the joining of the soul.

At the time of the flood we see this concept entirely lost. The depravity of those living then was very great. It is like all the rotten people / souls join together in sexual union against their Creator and were eternally destroyed because of their actions.

It was under these unfortunate circumstances that the world before the flood perished. Sins of stealing, adultery, lewdness, idolatry and mixing species brought on the destruction by flood. Having a sexual relationship with another person's spouse, is a form of stealing, but much worse! It is immoral! It is unforgivable. It is a form of idolatry, like leaving God for another. IT IS A VERY SERIOUS VIOLATION of The Torah and the Bible!!

Gematria And Mysticism In Genesis

Commandment Six:

Do Not Steal!

מִכֹּל עֵץ־הַגָּן
Mee Cohl   Aytz   Hah Gawn
From all the Trees in the Garden (EXCEPT)
308 = 50ן 3ג 5ה   90ץ 70ע   30ל 20כ 40מ

שׁוּב
Shoov
Return
308 = 2ב 6ו 300שׁ

Shoov – Return - Why would anyone need to return? What does the concept of return indicate? There is a place for everything. If something is out of place return it to it's place. There was only one tree in the entire Garden that the fruit could not be picked. The fruit must be left alone. Just picking the fruit was a form of taking, i.e. stealing. Say for example that Adam and Eve were not in the center of the Garden. They were somewhere else. Say the serpent brought the fruit to Adam and Eve. Their responsibility would be to return the fruit. However it appears like Adam and Eve were in the center of the garden standing near or siting close to the forbidden tree. Why would they come so close? I don't know! They were in the temptation area of the tree before the serpent came along...

Regardless we learn through this Gematria that we have a place where we belong. That place is close to God. If we have wandered away from that place we need to return. Every tree has its place in the Garden. Every fruit has its respective place on each tree. Everything had its place. Adam and Eve had their place. When they wondered from their place what happened?

מִכֹּל עֵץ־הַגָּן From all of the trees = {Prohibition against stealing} Mee Cawl - Aytz - Ha Gawn represents that Adam and Eve could eat from every tree in the Garden of Eden but one. They were prohibited from eating from the Tree of Knowledge of Good and Evil. When we take what is prohibited from us that action is stealing.

Within our home we have two beagle pups, Kaley and Dovi. There are times we place them on a leash so they can enjoy the freedom of running back and forth on a line in our yard. Then there are times we separate them by leash during mealtime and for other reasons. They can go anywhere they want within the limits of the leash. At other times Kaley and Dovi are not on the leash. They were allowed to run free. In cold weather they played in the garage or their bedroom.

Originally the garage and bedroom had a door to contain them so they could not wander at will throughout our home. After several weeks we established the bedroom just for rest time and the garage for play time. Now we frequently remove the door. Then the boys reached the age when they could understand a command. They were at a place where they had developed and where they understood the training commands. They understood the rest place, the play place and they understood that even though the door has been removed they are still not permitted to leave their area without permission. What is the point? Now that the door has been removed the boys have a choice. They can obey or they can disobey. At twelve weeks they knew the difference.

Now in a similar way God Established certain laws for Adam and Eve.

When the Lord God Commanded the man, *'You may certainly eat from every tree in the Garden. But from the Tree of Knowledge of what is good and evil, you shall not eat from it...'*, the way in which the Lord God Worded His Commandments established two categories:

First, 'what belongs to you {the man} and your wife is acceptable to eat.'

Second, 'What does not belong to you or your wife is not acceptable to eat.' By doing this the Lord God Establishes a series of laws, one of which, is do not take what does not belong to you or your wife. *'Do not steal.'*

When the man took from the tree, that was forbidden to him, he broke the Commandment *'Do Not Steal.'* He made the choice to take what did not belong to him.

אָכֹל תֹּאכֵל Eat freely = {Be kind to animals} Aw Chohl - Toh Chohl represented to Adam and Eve that they could eat freely of all plant life except the Tree of Knowledge of Good and Evil. This also meant they could not eat animals. However later, after the flood, Noah and his descendants would be permitted to eat animals, birds and fish. Yet this meant that one was required to gently take the life of an animal. It was and still is forbidden to remove limbs from living animals and eat them. The Torah considers such an action immoral and unkind to animals. The point is that one must take the kindest and most gentle approach to taking an animals life. The Torah prohibits all forms of rifle hunting, trapping and all but one form of bow hunting.

Gematria And Mysticism In Genesis

Commandment Seven:

Be Kind To Animals

אָכֹל תֹּאכֵל
Aw Cohl   Toh Cayhl
Eat Freely
502 = 30ל 20כ 1א 400ת   30ל 20כ 1א

בָּשָׂר
Baw Sawr Flesh
502 = 200ר 300שׁ 2ב

As we learn together in this book, we will face a point many may have not considered. The entire world including animals were vegetarians until 1657 after the flood. Remember Adam and Eve were only permitted to eat plant / tree life. The question must be asked. Why the serpent chose the tree in the middle of the Garden instead of a little calf or lamb? Killing one of them would be a sin. It would be disobedience to God. It would be murder. It would be stealing. Before the flood man was to be kind to animals. Man was not permitted to work animals. The earth was cursed because of Adam's sin. Why the earth? The dust of the ground was the physical parent from which Adam was taken. His soul could not be cursed because that was the perfect part within Adam and Eve. Yet notice that Adam was to work the soil. Nothing is said about using animals to ride or plow or haul etc. Mankind was to be kind to 'Flesh' / animals.

We have already shown in the first six Noach Commandments that up until the time of the flood man was prevented from shedding blood except for sacrifice. All mankind were vegetarians until after the flood. Now after the flood God Permits man to eat flesh providing he first removes the blood from the meat and providing he does not cut a limb from a living animal and eat it, Genesis 9.3.

The climate obviously had changed. The atmosphere had also changed. In addition, animals towards the end of life on earth before the flood began to rebel against God with unnatural mixes. As a result, after the flood everything became food for mankind. This was a judgment against unnatural mixes; first, angels and man and second, animals of one kind with animals of another kind.

They were Forbidden by God to mix.

Additional Information

There is a wealth of additional information like the following two examples that prove the existence of the Seven Noah Commandments.

In addition to the Seven Noah Commandments, history proves some information on several other forms of justice existing thousands of years back. Consider the Hammurabi Code and the Assyrian Laws which are both in excess of 3,800 years old and the Hittite Code which descended from Heth the great grandson of Noah. Each of these are shorter versions of the Seven Commandments.

Gematria And Mysticism In Genesis

Genesis Chapter 3
What the Bible Teaches About the Serpent ©

In chapter three we study about the original sin. We observe how sin is introduced. Sin is introduced by a cunning, crafty, clever, skilled, artful, devious, scheming, calculating, shrewd, astute, deceitful, deceptive serpent whose aim is to achieve a goal. The serpent wanted Eve for his partner.

Gematria And Mysticism In Genesis

Dear Ones, the Torah Says the sin of Adam and Eve came about through a talking serpent that could reason and lie.

Genesis 3.1
Now the serpent was more subtle than any beast of the field which the Lord God had Made, And he said to the woman, Has God Said, you shall not eat of every tree of the garden?

1.) Talking: Genesis 3.1
'And the serpent said...'

2.) Reasoning: Genesis 3.1
'Did God even say that you should not eat from the trees of the Garden?'

3.) Lies: Genesis 3.1
'You certainly will not die. For God Knows that on the day you will eat from it, your eyes will be opened, and you will become gods, knowing what is good and what is evil.'

4.) False Promises: Genesis 3.1

Gematria And Mysticism In Genesis

Why would the serpent say these Words, *'knowing what is good and what is evil'* Why would he say this when humankind were created with a Good Inclination and an Evil Inclination? וַיִּיצֶר [The word vah-yizer in Genesis 2.7] is written with two Yud's, to show that God Created two inclinations, one good and the other evil, Beresheit 61a.

Man already knew what was good and evil. The statement from the serpent indicates that humans were missing something. Was something missing in humankind?

5.) Listening to the wrong beings: Genesis 3.5

6.) Being Influenced by the wrong being:
Genesis 3.5
They were influenced by the serpent, whose cunning, crafty, clever, skilled, artful, devious, scheming, calculating, shrewd, astute, deceitful, deceptive ways enticed them to sin.

7.) Seeing: Genesis 3.6
וַתֵּרֶא The Woman saw... Notice the Letter Tav in front of the Letter ר Reish. The Tav is not part of

the normal word. The ת Tav is in this place to tell us this is an important sign and to investigate.
Genesis 3.6

וַתֵּרֶא הָאִשָּׁה כִּי טוֹב הָעֵץ

וַתֵּרֶא הָאִשָּׁה כִּי טוֹב הָעֵץ לְמַאֲכָל וְכִי תַאֲוָה־הוּא לָעֵינַיִם וְנֶחְמָד הָעֵץ לְהַשְׂכִּיל וַתִּקַּח מִפִּרְיוֹ וַתֹּאכַל וַתִּתֵּן גַּם־לְאִישָׁהּ עִמָּהּ וַיֹּאכַל׃

8.) Tempting: Genesis 3.6
The fruit was tempting. Sin is tempting. Disobedience is tempting.

9.) Appealing: Genesis 3.6 Sin is appealing.

10.) Obtaining Wisdom: Genesis 3.6
Yes, their eyes were opened. Yes, they obtained wisdom. They obtained wisdom that they could only experience from sinning.

After reviewing these points we will now review Adam and Eve's surroundings.

Gematria And Mysticism In Genesis

Genesis 1.27 clearly states,

וַיִּבְרָא אֱלֹהִים ׀ אֶת־הָאָדָם בְּצַלְמוֹ בְּצֶלֶם אֱלֹהִים
בָּרָא אֹתוֹ זָכָר וּנְקֵבָה בָּרָא אֹתָם :

'And the Lord God Created Everything from the Letter Aleph to the Letter Tav of Adam and Eve.' Nothing was left out. They were created complete. Their relationship was prepared for every situation. There was nothing they could not face. They were prepared to face sin from even the most cunning, crafty, clever, skilled, artful, devious, scheming, calculating, shrewd, astute, deceitful, deceptive serpent!

Genesis 1.27

וַיִּבְרָא אֱלֹהִים ׀ אֶת־הָאָדָם בְּצַלְמוֹ בְּצֶלֶם אֱלֹהִים
בָּרָא אֹתוֹ זָכָר וּנְקֵבָה בָּרָא אֹתָם

Why would *'knowing what is good and what is evil'* attract Eve to disobey the Command of the Creator in Genesis 2.7?

Did she want something that was out of her reach. Why would Adam follow her? Why does The

Torah Say, 'after they disobeyed God' *'that their eyes were opened that they realized that they were naked"*? (Genesis 3.7)

The Midrash discusses Adam and Eve's united responsibility to work and guard the Garden of Eden. At this chronological, i.e. when the man was placed in the garden, they were sharing the same body. This was before Eve was separated from Adam.

Genesis 2.15

וַיִּקַּח יְהֹוָה אֱלֹהִים אֶת־הָאָדָם וַיַּנִּחֵהוּ בְגַן־עֵדֶן לְעָבְדָהּ וּלְשָׁמְרָהּ׃

The Creator put the Adam (Adam and Eve) in the Garden to Work it and to guard it. Yet, Our Sages ask the question what were they to guard? What were they to care for? Everything that our Creator Created was made perfectly. They did not need to water. Four rivers flowed out of Garden of Eden. They did not need to pull weeds. Weeds were a result of a later sin. At that time trees and vines

Gematria And Mysticism In Genesis

did not require attention.

Our Sages Teach that Adam was Instructed to Guard meaning Observe The Torah. Rabbi Moshe Weissman, The Midrash Says (Brooklyn, New York: Benei Yakov Publications 1980), pp 42, 43

Adam was to care for the Observances given to him by the Creator from The Torah. The Sages Teach that the Tree of Life symbolizes The Torah. Adam and Eve were to eat from The Torah. The water flowing from the Garden of Eden symbolizes The Torah. Adam and Eve were to drink from the streams of The Torah. What Torah was man to learn and to observe? Man was to learn the Seven Laws which are binding upon all humanity. Rabbi Moshe Weissman, The Midrash Says (Brooklyn, New York: Benei Yakov Publications 1980), pp 43

However, there are many possibilities, including that the serpent was already in a fallen condition and as a result could not be trusted. It would appear that וּלְשָׁמְרָ Voo Lih Shah Mih Raw meaning to guard was intended specifically for the serpent. However we can Mystically see this is only a portion of the picture. The Gematria לְעָבְדָה Lih Aw Bih Dawh turns our attention in a different direction. We know that our Creator is Loving, Caring and Compassionate. Our Creator is a Just God. Our Creator would not Create Adam and Eve place them in the Garden without first Teaching and Instructing them in everything they needed to know. We see this in the Gematria 111. The Torah says Adam was placed in the Garden to work. This means Adam was trained in all aspects of the work that he would be required to perform. Adam was a completely capable individual. He wasn't ill trained.

Now, for those of us who may not understand, in those days, *'A mist went up from the earth, and watered the whole face of the ground,'* Genesis 2.6. In addition the Garden had four rivers flowing from it. The Torah says, *And a river went out from Eden to water the garden; and from there it was divided, and became four rivers,* Genesis 2.10. At this time the garden did not require weeding. There were no weeds until after Adam's sin. The thorns, thistles exist as part of the curse. *'__And to Adam he said, Because you have listened to the voice of your wife,__ and have eaten of the tree, of which I commanded you, saying, You shall not eat of it; cursed is the ground for your sake; in sorrow shall you eat of it all the days of your life; Thorns also and thistles shall it bring forth to you; and you shall eat the herb of the field; In the sweat of your face shall you eat bread, till you return to the ground; for out of it you were taken; for dust you are, and to dust shall you return,'* Genesis 3.17-19.

What I am trying to say is that the Garden was in pristine condition. This is not the type of work God intended for Adam. From day six forward there were two precious souls living on earth. A third precious soul would join Adam and Even before they were required to leave the Garden. These souls needed a Spiritual leader. Adam was selected to be that Spiritual leader. The type of work God Required from Adam was Spiritual. Adam was placed in the Garden to Minister to the Creator from the Holy Place, the separated Place in the Center of the Garden.

Dear Ones, our Creator separates people, places, and things for His Service. When our Creator does this we call that person, place or thing Sanctified or Holy. We call it Separated. The Tree in the center of the Garden was such a place. Our Creator Said that you shall not eat it. Our Creator Separated this from all other trees in the Garden. Our Creator Separated the Holy Land of Israel from all other lands. Israel is the Holy Land. Our Creator Separated Jerusalem from all the cities in the world. Jerusalem is the Holy City. Our Creator Separated the Jewish people from other people. We are known as the Holy people. In this same sense the center of the Garden was a Holy Place. It was Separated unto the Lord. It was there that Adam ministered to the Creator. The Aleph is the first Letter of the Aleph Bet, the Hebrew Aleph Bet. The Letter Aleph represents our Creator. The Gematria of the Aleph is 111.

אלף

The Aleph Represents God
111 = 80ף 30ל 1א

Gematria And Mysticism In Genesis

לְעָבְדָה
Lih Aw Bih Dawh
To Serve To Work
111 = 5ה 4ד 2ב 70ע 30ל

לְכַהֲנוֹ
Lih Cah Hih Noot
To Minister
111 = 6ו 50נ 5ה 20כ 30ל

A few pages ago we were discussing the Word וּלְשָׁמְרָה Ooh Lih Shaw Mih Rawh meaning to guard. In this instance the reference is to Guard and to Observe the Commands in the Torah. Let us pick up this theme again. The Gematria of וּלְשָׁמְרָה Ooh Lih Shaw Mih Rawh is 581. To a degree this Gematria is about the challenge of Guarding and Observing the Torah and human failing. Another Gematria speaks of Israel when it says 'from Israel'. This could be the long gap between when Adam Guarded the Torah up until the Children of Israel would be selected to Guard the Torah. From Adam The Children of Israel are next in line to be given the charge of Guarding and Observing the Torah.

וּלְשָׁמְרָה
Ooh Lih Shaw Mih Rawh
To Guard and To Observe
581= 5ה 200ר 40מ 300ש 30ל 6ו

מִיִשְׂרָאֵל
From Israel
581 = 30ל 1א 200ר 300ש 10י 40מ

A number of pages back I stated that it may appear like Adam's responsibility was to guard The Torah from the serpent. Let's look at the possibilities.

First, Adam was the Ruler of the World. Adam was the human King. The Adam was given power and authority over all forms of life on earth.
Genesis 2.19, 20
'And out of the ground the Lord God formed every beast of the field, and every bird of the air; and brought them to Adam to see what he would call them; and <u>whatever Adam called every living</u>

Gematria And Mysticism In Genesis

creature, that was its name. *And Adam gave names to all cattle, and to the bird of the air, and to every beast of the field;...'*

יִקְרָא־לוֹ הָאָדָם נֶפֶשׁ חַיָּה הוּא שְׁמוֹ׃

Notice that whatever the Adam Called (Summoned) each creature by, that Summons was it's Name. The Word יִקְרָא Yee Kih Raw means to call or to summon.

The concept of being summoned established the Adam's authority. The Adam had the power to order creatures to appear before him / her. He / She had the power to communicate with them. God Brought them to him / her. God Established The Adam's power.

Genesis 1.26
'...let them have dominion over the fish of the sea, and over the birds of the air, and over the cattle, and over all the earth, and over every creeping thing that creeps upon the earth...'

Please keep in mind that at this time both Adam and Eve were joined together in one body. At this time neither the Male Adam or the Female Adam was the total authority. **The Lord God Gave them dominion over the fish,** IT IS VERY IMPORTANT TO UNDERSTAND THIS. From later in the day we learn that the Male Adam is in charge. However at this chronological point this is not clear yet. When our Creator takes the Female Adam from the side of the male Adam this action gives the impression that the Male Adam is in charge. Then when our Creator brings the Female Adam to the Male Adam as his wife this supports that the Male Adam is in charge.

Think of how difficult it was. Adam went from being a Male and Female to being a male only. Eve went from sharing a physical body with her husband Adam to having her own body. They bonded as Male and Female in one body. They interacted as two people within one body. When the Creator Separated them this changed their Physical being from one body to two bodies. Their individual intellect changed from one body sharing two minds to each body having it's own individual mind.

What would this feel like? What kind of an impact would this have on them? I don't know. At this point they were no longer equal. Each would need to adjust to their new rolls. The Male Adam was the Ruler of the entire world. Adam was the Holy Priest of the world. His responsibility was to minister from the holy place in the center of the Garden. His responsibility was to Guard and to Observe.

Now Eve also had a great deal of adjustment. Eve participated in calling the creatures and issuing each a name. She participated in authority over them. What was Eve's role in the newly formed authoritative structure? What were her responsibilities?

Genesis 2.18
The Creator Said, *'...It is not good for The Adam to be alone. I will construct an Aizer / Help mate for him...'*

Eve's role is clear. Eve is to assist Adam. How? As Ruler? No. As Priest? No! God Gives Eve one of

His Attributes. The Creator Gives Eve the Attribute of Tiferet / Beauty. Within the Sefirot our Sages diagram the emanations of our Creator so that we will better understand our Creator. Tiferet is in the center. Tiferet is balanced. Kindness on the right of Tiferet and Strength on the left. How do we know Our Creator Gave Beauty to Eve? Sages say, God adorned her like a bride. He braided her hair and brought her to Adam. Our Creator constructed the marriage Chupah for the marriage ceremony. The Holy One, Blessed be He, took a cup of wine and blessed them. Michael and Gabriel were Adam's 'best men'. Eve was very beautiful. See B R 18.1 - Rabbi Meir Zlotowitz and Rabbi Nosson Scherman, The Artscroll Tanach Series - Bereishis Vol. I(a) (Brooklyn, New York: Mesorah Publications, Ltd. 3rd Impression, 1989), pp 109 - 111

This tells us of her role as a leader then. Her position was center. Eve was the buffer. Eve was not the authority. Her responsibility was one of balance. Her responsibility was to be in the center. Where was the Tree of Knowledge of Good and Evil? The Tree was in the center of the Garden. Eve's role was known throughout the universe. She was the buffer between Creation and Adam. If a creature had an issue they would approach Eve. She would act as a mediator as a buffer between Adam and Creation. This was prior to the sin.

The serpent could see this. The Torah Says the serpent was cunning. The serpent devised a plan to use the system against them.

The serpent presents a problem to Eve. Adam is not involved. It might be a little like one branch of government does not communicate well with the other. I don't know!

The Serpent Inquires:
Perhaps, God said, you shall not eat of every tree of the garden?

Eve:
We may eat of the fruit of the trees of the garden; But of the fruit of the tree which is in the midst of the garden. God has said, you shall not eat of it, nor shall you touch it, lest you die.

The Serpent argues:

Surely you shall not die. For God knows that in the day you eat of it, then your eyes shall be opened, and you shall be as gods, knowing good and evil.

Eve investigates the matter.
She discovers the Tree is good to eat even though she did not taste the Tree yet. Eve observes the Tree was a delight to the eyes. Why didn't she notice this before? Eve notices the Tree was desirable as a means to Wisdom.

She reaches out takes the fruit and takes a bite.

Genesis 3.2-7
And [the serpent] said to the woman, Has God Said, you shall not eat of every tree of the garden? And the woman said to the serpent, We may eat of the fruit of the trees of the garden; But of the fruit of the tree which is in the midst of the garden, God Has Said, you shall not eat of it, nor shall you touch it, lest you die. And the serpent said to the woman, surely you shall not die; For God Knows that in the day you eat of it, then your eyes shall be opened, and you shall be as gods, knowing good

and evil, And when the woman saw that the tree was good for food, and that it was pleasant to the eyes, and a tree to be desired to make one wise, she took of its fruit, and ate, <u>and gave also to her husband with her; and he ate.</u> And the eyes of them both were opened, and they knew that they were naked; and they sewed fig leaves together, and made themselves aprons.

Where was Adam? He was right there with Eve. Why didn't Adam get involved? Adam was King. Adam was Ruler. Adam was priest? Why didn't Adam command the serpent to be quiet? Adam's responsibility was to listen. He was to hear the complaint then to rule on it. Adam had to be fair. He had to be just! Think of it like this. If we came to our Creator with an issue and we were misrepresenting the Truth and we were mixing truth with lies etc. and the Creator told us to be quiet and to return to our job or our home etc. Would we feel like that was just? Would we feel like our issues had been heard? I don't think so. Yes, Adam had the power as did Eve to put a stop to this at any point. But in their roles they were trying to be fair and just and got caught in the craftiness of the serpent.

Please note the sixth, seventh and eighth Words back in Genesis 2.19 which follows.

כָּל־חַיַת הַשָּׂדֶה Cawl meaning כָּל 'All' חַיַת Chah Yaht meaning 'Beast or Life' הַשָּׂדֶה Hah Saw Deh, meaning of the cultivated field.

Genesis 2.19

וַיִּצֶר יְהֹוָה אֱלֹהִים מִן־הָאֲדָמָה כָּל־חַיַת הַשָּׂדֶה וְאֵת כָּל־עוֹף הַשָּׁמַיִם וַיָּבֵא אֶל־הָאָדָם לִרְאוֹת מַה־יִּקְרָא־לוֹ וְכֹל אֲשֶׁר יִקְרָא־לוֹ הָאָדָם נֶפֶשׁ חַיָּה הוּא שְׁמוֹ:

We compare Genesis 2.19 to Genesis 3.1. This defines the serpent as having been Made / Formed out of the ground by the Lord God. He was a beast of the field, based upon Genesis 2.19 and 3.1 In this instance, this simply means the serpent breathed. In this sense this is not a species. Yet it appears like it may be a species. This would

Gematria And Mysticism In Genesis

explain the serpents sexual desire for Eve. Based upon The Torah's definition both Adam and Eve were breathing. Yet they were from the human species not an animal species. Our Sages teach that the serpent lusted after Eve after watching Adam and Eve enjoying sexual relations. Remember they were not clothed. The Torah informs us, 'they were both naked, the man and his wife, and were not ashamed, Genesis 2.25. Rabbi Meir Zlotowitz and Rabbi Nosson Scherman, The Artscroll Tanach Series - Bereishis Vol. I(a) (Brooklyn, New York: Mesorah Publications, Ltd. 3rd Impression, 1989), p 112

And the וְהַנָּחָשׁ serpent was more עָרוּם subtle from any beast of the field which the Lord God had made. Let's note the words הַנָּחָשׁ meaning a snake or a serpent. Note the slight spelling difference between being naked עֲרוּמִּים or cunning עָרוּם .

The serpent was naked. Adam and Eve were naked. The serpent was cunning. Naked and cunning similar.
Genesis 3.1

וְהַנָּחָשׁ הָיָה עָרוּם מִכֹּל חַיַּת הַשָּׂדֶה אֲשֶׁר עָשָׂה

Gematria And Mysticism In Genesis

יְהוָֹה אֱלֹהִים וַיֹּאמֶר אֶל־הָאִשָּׁה אַף כִּי־אָמַר
אֱלֹהִים לֹא תֹאכְלוּ מִכֹּל עֵץ הַגָּן :1

The next point of interest is that the beasts of the field each had mates. Where was the serpent's mate? Adam and Eve named him and his mate serpent, i.e. נָחָשׁ .

What we have just discussed happened very fast. The majority of this happened on the sixth day. Adam and Eve were Created, Separated, Wed, Birthed Children, Administrated the World. Ministered as Priest and sinned, were judged and were punished all on the sixth day. Think about it.

This was a test. Think about what kind of test this was. They failed. They sinned. Were Adam and Eve being tested or was repentance being tested. There are different types of sin. Adam and Eve's sin is one of a different nature. They were punished yet it is a sin all of us can relate to. I think we can understand perhaps why they sinned. I cannot imagine anyone under similar circumstances doing better even though they may. This was their first day on the job. This was their first day of marriage. This was their first day of parenthood... This was their first day of life. Think about all that was happening in their world. They sinned they were punished of their sins. However in Genesis Chapter Four we learn how to deal with our sin in a meaningful way.

This was also a test to see if repentance would work. Repentance worked.

God took Adam and Eve. God placed them in the Garden. They had to deal with the serpent. Neither dealt well with the serpent. They individually failed. They failed as a couple. Adam was very angry about this even though he participated in the entire experience. He was right there next to her. He was in part responsible. He could have spoken to Eve. He could have spoken to the serpent. It appears like he did nothing but let it happen. This is not to suggest he should have dominated his wife as if he were in control of her. Yet, Adam could have spoken with Eve. He could have influenced Eve by perhaps discussing the Command the Lord God gave them.

Each of us will be tested. None of us will slide by without being tested. We will not get by the test. We will all be tested!

Each of us will be tested. How do I know we will be tested? Adam and Eve were made of dust. The serpent was cursed by our Creator. Our Creator Said to the serpent, '...*upon your belly shall you go, and dust shall you eat all the days of your life...*' This means that even though, the serpent now crawls... and the serpent cannot speak... and the serpent cannot have intellectual conversations with you, the serpent is still crawling around through the dust of our lives, and as a result we must be careful. We do not need to be afraid. We need to be careful!! We have everything we need to pass the test.

Spirituality acknowledges the existence of two forces within each of us. Both forces were created by God. These forces are called Yetzer Tov meaning the good inclination and Yetzer Raw meaning the bad inclination. Each of us has an original operating system with a Yetzer Tov and a Yetzer Raw. Both are equal. The function of the Yetzer Tov is to follow and to Observe what God has Commanded. The function of the Yetzer Raw is to challenge us to disobey God's Commandments... to challenge our desire to love and honor God. The Yetzer Raw is not a demon or a devil. It is our tester...

A side note about Satan.

Dear ones, certain religions have created this huge fear of Satan. They picture Satan as the devil, as a demon or as the serpent in the Garden of Eden. These religious teachings depict Satan as evil. They claim that the conclusion of Satan and his followers will be eternal death... destruction and hellfire.

Dear Ones, God Created the Suton {Satan} as a tester. The purpose of Suton can be easily understood by the following two examples. First, before a jet is approved to carry passengers it must be tested. It is not enough to accept the word of the engineers or the manufacturer regarding the safety or performance of the jet. The jet must pass a series of tests to prove it's air worthiness.

Nothing short of testing the commercial jet will suffice. As a result our government has designed a series of tests that each jet / each plane must pass before it is certified for passenger use. From the consumer's viewpoint testing is very good. We want to feel safe when we fly. The consumer supports strict airline standards. The consumer wants frequent checks. The consumer wants frequent tests...

Second, when one applies for employment one often sends a resume along with an employment application. What is the purpose of the resume and the application? It is to demonstrate one's qualifications to the potential employer. If the applicant's resume and application are accepted, an interview is normally set. Sometimes a second and third interview are required. Why? Each are series of tests that determine one's ability. Now, dear reader, religions do not question the purpose for testing jet airliners or potential employees. Why then don't religions make this connection in a person's daily life? Why do religions associate problems in the neighborhood, at school or on the job with Satan? Why do they teach that one must rebuke Satan? Readers, Spirituality realizes the purpose for Suton. We understand that God Created Suton for the purpose of testing us. We understand the allegiance of our Yetzer Raw and Suton. We understand, put simply, that the concept of the Yetzer Raw is like that of a commercial jet or a job applicant. So that given the situation we live with an appreciation for the purpose of our Yetzer Raw and for the Suton provides that insight. Both are agents of God designed to test and to prove us. So when the Spiritualist has problems in the neighborhood, at school or on the job the Spiritualist understands it is a test to prove one's dedication to observe what God has Commanded. One does not rebuke the tester, one accepts the challenge to remain committed to what God has Commanded.

Now a final word about Suton. God created Suton for the purpose of testing us. Suton is NOT some fallen, sinful angel. Suton is not going to burn in hell for fulfilling God's Commands. Testing us is the responsibility of Suton. There is a great difference here between the serpent, the snake of Genesis 3 and Suton which was Created by God to test us. The serpent was punished because the serpent did wrong. The serpent was intent on testing Adam and Eve beyond reasonable limits. The serpent lied about the end result and the consequences.

Gematria And Mysticism In Genesis

Dear reader, if one cheats on their income taxes there are penalties. If one steals there are penalties. If one does wrong there are penalties. The Suton knows and acknowledges these penalties. The Suton understands that there is a limit to the scope of testing. On the other hand, the serpent exceeded these limits. As a result, speech and reason were removed from the serpent. As a result the serpent was removed from a lofty position to the very lowest position.

Understanding this Spiritualist / Judaic concept carries the highest requirements of integrity, honesty and truthfulness among religious leaders and teachers. We must be so careful not to misstate or misdirect our students, our colleagues, et al. God Exacts great penalties for knowingly misrepresenting what God has Said, as the serpent did.

The Malachim {angels} that were permitted to visit earth with the Creator's sanction exceeded their limits. The Midrash records the argument of Shamchazai and Azael, two angels who believed they could sanctify God's name on earth greater than man could. The Creator permitted them to try to prove their claim knowing they would fail. They did fail. Yet they needed an even playing field where they could rise or fall on their own. The Torah records that the earth was destroyed because of them {Shamchazai and Azael}, Genesis 6:13. However 120 years were provided for anyone who wanted to repent. No one repented. Shamchazai and Azael and all the evil people of the earth were destroyed.

The nature of the Yetzer Raw is not to deny the penalties or the existence of limits. In our heart of hearts we know what is right and what is wrong! The nature of the Yetzer Raw is to disobey what God has Commanded, knowing that it is wrong. Yet the Yetzer Raw is not fooled or surprised when penalties are required for sin. The Yetzer Raw understands limits and when the limits are exceeded.

The Suton presents the challenges for us to obey or to disobey. The challenges are presented skillfully yet within limits. Hah Naw Chawsh did not observe these limits. Remember all tests are on an even playing field. Again we are reminded that prior to the flood of Noah the hearts of men were continually evil {Genesis 6:5}. So while we don't want to dwell on their destruction we must acknowledge the possibility for failure and the consequences of failure. The potential for failure must be real, otherwise the test would not be valid. Even though we are all subject to the tests of our own Yetzer Raw in conjunction with Suton, it is just as easy for us to pass a test as it is to fail a test. The same effort is required to succeed as to fail. God's intention is for us to be successful! We have all the tools to be successful! No person is created or born with a greater advantage. God is fair! God is just! So, dear ones, be encouraged with your potential for success.

Do not fear Suton or your Yetzer Raw. Scale the mountain! Be successful! Be happy! Do not fear the descriptions other religions paint of Suton or Suton's power to destroy. Do not be fearful from their claims and threats of hellfire and damnation. God loves us! Love God! Love each other! Accept tests in their proper perspective! Succeed!

Seven things were created before the world was created, and these are they: The Torah, repentance, the Garden of Eden, Gehenna, the Throne of Glory, the Temple, and the name of the Messiah.

The Torah, for it is written, *'The Lord Made me [sc. the Torah] as the beginning of his way...' Proverbs 8.22*

Gematria And Mysticism In Genesis

Repentance, for it is written, 'Before the mountains were brought forth, and it is written, You turn man to contrition, and saying, Repent, you the children of men. Pesach 54a

Psalms 90.2, 3

בְּטֶרֶם ׀ הָרִים יֻלָּדוּ וַתְּחוֹלֵל אֶרֶץ וְתֵבֵל וּמֵעוֹלָם עַד־עוֹלָם אַתָּה אֵל:

תָּשֵׁב אֱנוֹשׁ עַד־דַּכָּא וַתֹּאמֶר שׁוּבוּ בְנֵי־אָדָם:

'Before the mountains were brought forth, before you had formed the earth and the world, from everlasting to everlasting, you are God. **You turn man back** *to dust; and Saying* **Repent, O children of men,'** Psalm 90.2, 3.

Moses Taught in Psalms Ninety that Repentance was Created before the earth and the world were formed. What does this say about Repentance.

From before Creation our Creator welcomed Repentance / Return to God 24 / 7. Adam the First Man wrote a book entitled Sefer Raziel Ha Malach meaning The Book [Given to me by] the Angel

Raziel. In his book Adam discusses his prayer for repentance after sinning. After leaving the Garden Adam prayed for three days. Adam Said, 'I realize that I have sinned. Because of my sin I was banished from the Garden of Eden... The animals do not fear me... Forgive me...' After three days of prayer an Angel brought Adam a message from the Creator. 'Your prayers have been accepted.'

Dear Ones from the minute Adam began to pray God Acknowledged his prayers. Two Books of Interest: Avraham Yaakov Finkel, <u>Kabbalah</u> (Southfield, Mi, Targum, Nanuet NY, Feldheim Publishers, 2002) and Rabbi Arey Kaplan, (San Francisco, CA 500 3rd Street Suite 230 Red Wheel / Weiser LLC 1997) Sefer Yetzirah – The Book of Creation.

Exodus 34.6, 7

יְהֹוָה ׀ יְהֹוָה אֵל רַחוּם וְחַנּוּן אֶרֶךְ אַפַּיִם וְרַב־חֶסֶד וֶאֱמֶת:
נֹצֵר חֶסֶד לָאֲלָפִים נֹשֵׂא עָוֹן וָפֶשַׁע וְחַטָּאָה ...

The Lord, The Lord God, [our God is] merciful and gracious, long suffering, and abundant in goodness and truth, [He] Keeps Mercy for thousands, forgiving iniquity and transgression and sin...

Gematria And Mysticism In Genesis

It is important to understand that from before Creation God established repentance for all His Creation and that God Forgives Sin and that God has been forgiving sin from the time of Adam and Eve forward. Sinful humans need the Creator's forgiveness. We will discuss how one deals with sin, and how God Forgives sin later in Genesis Chapter 4.

Gematria And Mysticism In Genesis

Genesis Chapter 4
What is a Man's Responsibility to His Wife?

What was the relation between Adam and Eve in light of what The Torah Shares with us. For many years their relationship was greatly strained. They lived apart for 130 years after the death of Abel.

Dear Ones, Chapter Four begins with, *And the man knew [sexually experienced] everything from the Letter Aleph to Tav of Chavah / Eve, his wife...* This means they experienced everything sexual. I'm not saying they experienced 'every sexual pleasure'. It seems they may have gone beyond sexual pleasure. They may have experienced things which were not sexual pleasures. I don't know!

Genesis 4.1

וְהָאָדָם יָדַע אֶת־חַוָּה אִשְׁתּוֹ
וַתַּהַר וַתֵּלֶד אֶת־קַיִן
וַתֹּאמֶר קָנִיתִי אִישׁ אֶת־יְהוָה׃

Genesis 4.1

And the man knew [physically experienced] everything from the Letter Aleph to Tav of Chavah / Eve, his wife and she became pregnant and birthed **everything from Aleph to Tav of Cain...** *and she said, from everything from Aleph to Tav of the Lord I have Possessed / Acquired a man.*

Gematria And Mysticism In Genesis

The Word ידע / Yaw Dah means to know or to learn. Yaw Dah is followed by the Word את / Eht meaning 'everything from the first Letter of the Aleph Bet, the Letter Aleph to the last Letter of the Aleph Bet, the Letter Tav. *The Torah Says Adam knew… and Adam sexually experienced everything from Aleph to Tav of Eve.* The Torah does not Say what Eve knew or what Eve sexually experienced.

It is most important to inquire why The Torah Defines Eve as 'his wife'. Who else could be his wife? Why does The Torah Express that Eve was 'his wife'? Why does The Torah Say he knew, he experienced sexual pleasure? Was this all about Adam? What about Eve?

Then Eve's Statement after giving birth is unique. Eve Says, I acquired a man through the Lord. I translate this as the Lord acquired a man for me. There are sexual overtones to the name Cain. The meaning of name קין Cain is big testicles or spear. Yet we know the name of Cain is most likely a derivative of Eve's comment קניתי Kaw Nee Tee, as in the Lord acquired a man for me. The shoresh / root Word for קניתי Kaw Nee Tee is קנה Kaw Nawh meaning acquire or possess. When one acquires something it is their possession. How did Adam possess Eve?

Dear ones, Cain was born in the Garden of Eden. Cain was born before the sixth day concluded. Cain was born before Adam and Eve / His Father and Mother were removed from the Garden of Eden. Remember Chapter three's discussion pointed to the man being removed from Garden of Eden and not the woman.

The Torah Says, the Lord God Sent him out... Genesis 3.23. The Torah Says, He banished the man [from Garden of Eden]... Genesis 3.24. In the last lesson I asked why Eve left the Garden of Eden. In this lesson I ask why did Cain leave the Garden of Eden? Cain was conceived through the sexual acts of his father. What were those sexual acts?

Our Sages Teach that when a man and women have sex that they should concentrate on holiness and purity and thoughts of God and The Torah and the Observances of The Torah. What was Adam thinking when he engaged physically with Eve? What thoughts passed through his mind? I don't know. What was Eve thinking when she was possessed by Adam? What passed through her mind? I don't know. Their union resulted in Cain. The world was destroyed because of Cain and his descendants.

We are going to discuss Cain for a few pages then return to the discussion on relationships.

The Gematria of קַיִן is 160. The Gematria of נָפָל Naw Phawl meaning fallen is also the Gematria 160. Decades down the road the Giants, which were the offspring of the fallen angels, were called the fallen. The fallen angels and the giants had relationships with the daughters of men and produced unusual children.

קַיִן
Cain
160= 50ן 10י 100ק

נָפַל
Fallen
160 = 30ל 80פ 50נ

Genesis 6.4

הַנְּפִלִים הָיוּ בָאָרֶץ בַּיָּמִים הָהֵם וְגַם אַחֲרֵי־כֵן אֲשֶׁר יָבֹאוּ בְּנֵי הָאֱלֹהִים אֶל־בְּנוֹת הָאָדָם וְיָלְדוּ לָהֶם הֵמָּה הַגִּבֹּרִים אֲשֶׁר מֵעוֹלָם אַנְשֵׁי הַשֵּׁם׃

הַנְּפִלִים Ha Nih Fee Leem means 'The Fallen'.

Rabbi Meir Zlotowitz and Rabbi Nosson Scherman, <u>The Artscroll Tanach Series - Bereishis Vol. I(a)</u> (Brooklyn, New York: Mesorah Publications, Ltd. 3rd Impression, 1989), p184

In addition to the fallen angels, the giants were the *'mighty who, from old were men of devastation'*, Genesis 6.4. It is possible one was the transmigration of Cain. We see the potential tie in with the Words אֶת־קַיִן meaning *'everything from Aleph to Tav of Cain...'* This would certainly include Cains descendants. It could also include Cain in a reincarnated state.

Gematria And Mysticism In Genesis

Genesis 6.18

*But with you **I will establish** my covenant; and you shall come into the ark, you, and your sons, and your wife, and your sons' wives with you.*

Any claim to the covenant by the descendants of Cain was being removed by the Creator at the time of the flood and destruction of the world. How could Cain or his descendants make a claim of the Creator's Covenant? Cain was the first born. The Priesthood would have passed from Adam to Cain and onto Cain's firstborn Enoch. However everyone of Cain's descendants were destroyed in the Noah Flood... with one exception. Og King of Bashan. Our Sages teach that he was one of the 'Fallen' who survived the Noah flood by climbing on board the ark and sitting atop the Ark. Noach drilled a hole through the wood and fed Og through this hole. Og was a descendant of a daughter of Cain and a fallen angel. He became the King of Bashan who the Children of Israel would kill in battle before entering the Holy Land. These are fine details that are significant. Og was a direct descendant of Cain, he survived the flood.

So we understand one possible reason for our Creator to set forth His Will וַהֲקִמֹתִי Vah Hah Kee Moh Tee meaning I will Establish my Covenant with you... Pesach 61a

Genesis 6.17, 18

And, behold, I, myself, bring a flood of waters upon the earth, to destroy all flesh, where there is the breath of life, from under heaven; and every thing that is in the earth shall die. But with you, **I will establish my covenant;** *and you shall come into the ark, you, and your sons, and your wife, and your sons' wives with you.*

Og did not die. Og did not come into the Ark either. Still, the Covenant was established with Noah and his children. Our Creator was establishing the Rules on the Ark and in the new world. Another connection to the accountability of life. Og was outside the Ark. Og came from a lawless world to a world of laws. Og was not blessed by the Creator. He was not from the righteous line of Adam and Seth. Yet our Creator Gives this Instruction that remains intact for today.

Gematria And Mysticism In Genesis

Genesis 9.1-7

1.And God Blessed Noah and his sons, and said to them, Be fruitful, and multiply, and replenish the earth. 2 And the fear of you and the dread of you shall be upon every beast of the earth, and upon every bird of the air, upon all that moves upon the earth, and upon all the fishes of the sea; to your hand are they delivered. 3 Every moving thing that lives shall be food for you; even as the green herb have I given you all things. 4 But flesh with its life, which is its blood, you shall not eat. 5 And surely the blood of your lives **I will require;** *at the hand of every beast I will require it, and at the hand of man; at the hand of every man's brother I will require the life of man. 6 Whoever sheds man's blood, by man shall his blood be shed; for in the image of God he made man.*

The point here is that murder was forbidden. Killing animals properly was not forbidden. After killing the animal the blood must be removed from the flesh. However there are several other types of shedding blood that are capital offenses. Rape is one. Rape spills the blood of the victim and the victims child. All the survivors of the prior world were acquainted with the vileness of those living then. That type of evil was forbidden. Our Creator was establishing some rules where the past could not spill over into the future. We are discussing the establishment and maintenance of proper relationships.

אֶדְרְשֶׁנּוּ Ay Dih Rih Sheh Noo meaning I will require it.

אֶת־קַיִן
'everything from Aleph to Tav of Cain...'
561 = 50ן 10י 100ק   400ת 1א

וַהֲקִמֹתִי
Vah Hah Kee Moh
I will Establish
561 = 10י 400ת 40מ 100ק 5ה 6ו

אֶדְרְשֶׁנּוּ
Ay Dih Rih Sheh Noo
I will require it.

Gematria And Mysticism In Genesis

561 = 1ו 50נ 300ש 200ר 4ד 1א

Genesis 9.5
And surely your blood of your lives will I require; at the hand of every beast will I require it, and at the hand of man; at the hand of every man's brother will I require the life of man.

We have just been discussing Cain and his descendants for pages and how they and the fallen angels were responsible for the evil in the world. We began this discussion by asking the question, what was Adam thinking, when he and Eve were engaged in a physical relationship, and what was Eve thinking when she and Adam were engaged in a physical relationship? The point is that sex is not just about sex. Sex is about creating a little baby who will grow up one day. Sex is about putting the right kind of thoughts and energy into that creation that is happening between two people. Sex is NOT about the fulfillment of lust!! Sex is not about stealing another individual's spouse. Sex is not about rape!! Sex is not about a one night fling. I know people who have a half dozen children, each through a different partner. That is gross!! What kind of a life is this? Look at the old world that was destroyed. Look at the products from those multiple sinful relationships. Look at the children. **What kind of a child do you want to have?**

When The Torah Says Adam knew and Adam sexually experienced, it appears that the תפארת Tiferet / Beauty is missing. What did Eve experience? Where is the meeting in the center? Where is Tiferet? Where are the two married partners coming together to create? This will become more apparent as we study further. Where is the tranquility we began discussing?

The second son, Havel's name means to become vain. The name Havel points to his death. It would appear that all existence of Havel would be in vain because Cain would murder him.

What was the difference between the births of Cain and Hevel? Eve did not experience birth pain when Cain was born. Eve experienced birth pains when Hevel was born. After the birth of Hevel Adam and Eve separated for 130 years. Our Sages teach that Adam was angry with Eve.

During that 130 years Cain brought much evil into the world. It was necessary for Adam and Eve to get it right the next time they had a child. They needed to have more children so that the world would be populated with good. They really needed to concentrate on the act of procreating a Holy Child. Adam learned the importance of bringing good children into the world when he joined with Eve again.

Maybe it was good that Adam and Eve took sometime apart until they could get their issues worked out.

Adam saw that Abel was dead, Cain was cursed, and Cain's descendants had gone in evil ways. He knew his wife again - after a separation of 130 years (Midrash) - to ensure that worthwhile fore bearers of mankind would be produced (Malbim).
Rabbi Meir Zlotowitz and Rabbi Nosson Scherman, The Artscroll Tanach Series - Bereishis Vol. I(a) (Brooklyn, New York: Mesorah

Publications, Ltd. 3rd Impression, 1989), pp 163, 164

For 130 years evil grew. **Cain had almost choked out the hope of righteousness by killing his brother. Then Adam refused to have a relationship with Eve. These two factors almost eliminated us and any hope of righteousness.** Remember all of Cain's descendants perished in the flood.

Cain was not a good person. Yet he had a chance to be good.

Dear Ones, in Genesis 4 we experience our first discussion about sin and repentance in the Bible. Even though we know Adam and Eve sinned in Chapter Three, yet there is no talk about their repentance. Our Sages teach that the Lord God Created repentance before he Created the universe. We discussed this in Chapter three. We know repentance worked because The Torah Says, in Genesis 1.31 מְאֹד טוֹב Tov Mih Ood meaning 'Greatly Good or Extremely Good! We could say that the world was the proper oasis to have and

Gematria And Mysticism In Genesis

raise children. The Gematria for טוֹב מְאֹד is 62. This is also the Gematria for בְּנֵי Bih Nay meaning sons or children. In other words our goal should be to bring children into the best spiritual, mental and physical setting as possible.

Genesis 1.31

וַיַּרְא אֱלֹהִים אֶת־כָּל־אֲשֶׁר עָשָׂה וְהִנֵּה־טוֹב מְאֹד וַיְהִי־עֶרֶב וַיְהִי־בֹקֶר יוֹם הַשִּׁשִּׁי:

And God saw every thing that he had made, and, behold, it was extremely good. And there was evening and there was morning, the sixth day.

טוֹב מְאֹד
Tov Mih Ood
'Greatly Good or Extremely Good!
62 = 4ד 1א 40מ   2ב 6ו 9ט

בְּנֵי
Bih Nay

Sons or Children.
62 = 10י 50נ 2ב

Dear Ones, this was AFTER Adam and Eve sinned. It could not be good if they had not repented. Yet The Torah does not go into details about their repentance. Our Creator calls this Tov Mih Ood 'Greatly Good or Extremely Good!

Dear Ones, The Creator Provided a covering for Adam and Eve. They were naked. They needed a covering. The covering was not for their sin. They repented of their sin. Our Creator took lamb's wool and goat hair and braided it with snake skin. Our Sages teach that our Creator took these three items to design very special garments to cover and protect our first parents. The protection was necessary because the animals who did not sin were now forced into a world of sin. All creation was angry with Adam and Eve. NOTHING at all is said about offering a sacrifice.

The Torah says God Took skins. These were snake skins. Why? Our Creator forbid the taking of life. Humankind did not eat animals or birds or fish. We ate products of the ground. We were vegetarians until 1657 F C [From Creation]. - It is at this time our Creator Says, *'Every living thing shall be food for you...'* Genesis 9. Rabbi Moshe Weissman, The Midrash Says (Brooklyn, New York: Benei Yakov Publications 1980), p. 58

Up until this time it was forbidden to take even animal life.

The Torah shares the discussion about the punishment for Adam and Eve's sin. Yet we Observe two areas that point to their repentance in addition to Adams book discussing his repentance.

Here in Genesis 4 we deal with sin. Cain was a farmer. He brought a grain offering. That is fine. God loves grain offerings. We are taught his offering had issues. The issue with Cain's offering was it was spoiled flax seed. Cain did not bring the best of his fields. He did not bring the first of his fruits. God was not pleased with Cain's offering. On the other hand, Able brought the the best spun wool and goats hair. He brought the best cream and the best cheese. They were the best of his flocks crop. They were from his flocks first fruits. God was greatly pleased with his offering. Rabbi Nosson Scherman, <u>The Stone Edition The Chumash</u> (Mesorah Publications, Ltd., Brooklyn, N.Y. 1993), pp 21, 22.

Cain sinned. He did not offer God his best. Cain did not offer God his first fruits. The Lord God Came to have a talk with Cain. The emphasis of the talk was upon improvement and controlling one's evil inclination. The Torah Says,
Genesis 4.7

וְאִם לֹא תֵיטִיב לַפֶּתַח חַטָּאת רֹבֵץ

And 'if' you do not do well, i.e if you do not improve yourself sin Chah Tawt meaning sin חַטָּאת *creeps at the door.*

וְאֵלֶיךָ תְּשׁוּקָתוֹ וְאַתָּה תִּמְשָׁל־בּוֹ

It's desire is toward you, yet you can conquer it.

The Bible Teaches that we have power over the desires that bring about sin in each of our lives. Nothing is said about needing a redeemer or a savior. The Word וְאֵלֶיךָ Vih Ay Leh Chaw means 'to you or towards you'. The Word Vih Ah Taw means 'yet you...' The LORD is Teaching Cain that he has the ability to control his desires and to conquer them. This is how we deal with issues. The LORD Gives each of us strength to conquer our desires. This is God's Plan and has ALWAYS been God's Plan. If God is willing, I plan to discuss this in an up coming book entitled <u>God's Plan From The Beginning</u>.

Our sages teach that Adam, the first man *After a period of time...* [spoke to his sons about offering sacrifices.] Genesis 3.3 Adam indicated that at a time in the future the upcoming date would be Passover. He explained to his sons that the Children of Israel would bring a Paschal sacrifice that would be favorably received by the Lord. Our sages state that in doing this, he taught his sons, this is a propitious time for each of you to bring a sacrifice to God, and He will be pleased with you...

Gematria And Mysticism In Genesis

Rabbi Meir Zlotowitz and Rabbi Nosson Scherman, The Artscroll Tanach Series - Bereishis Vol. I(b) (Brooklyn, New York: Mesorah Publications, Ltd. 3rd Impression, 1989), p 144

As indicated earlier, Abel brought the best of his first fruits, and Cain brought spoiled flax seed. God Accepted Abel's offering and reject Cain's offering. Rabbi Nosson Scherman, The Stone Edition The Chumash (Mesorah Publications, Ltd., Brooklyn, N.Y. 1993), pp 21, 22

Even though this is what appears to be at the center of the issue, our Sages tell us there was something more. Cain was born with one twin sister. Abel was born with two twin sisters. Cain as the oldest brother wanted one of Abel's twin sisters for his wife. Abel maintained that Cain's twin sister was his wife and that his twin sisters were his wives. **Sefer HaYashar** (Hoboken, NJ: KTAV Publishing House, Inc., 1993) p.8 Rabbi Dr. H. Freedman, Midrash Rabba (New York, NY: The Soncino Press 1983) - Midrash Rabbah writes, Bereisheit p 181

Here again, we come back to a consistent problem that began with Cain. Cain murdered his brother to take Abel's twin sisters for his wives. When Cain murdered his brother Abel, this put the entire world in a downward spiral. It was dark and depressing. Now, who would bring good children into the world? Since Adam refused to make up with Eve this downward spiral continued. Then one day...

[Lamech] summoned [his wives] to their marital duties [after he accidentally murdered Cain]. They said to him: *Tomorrow a flood will come — are we to bear children for a curse?* [They were concerned that their children would be cursed or punished like Cain. They saw no point in having children.]

They all came to Adam and presented their case to him. Lemech's wives argued, *Our master, our husband killed our great-grandfather Cain and our son Tuval Cain. Why should we continue to bear additional children who are doomed to annihilation?*

Lemech said, *My master, it all happened by accident and was not done intentionally.* Adam decided, *Listen to your husband, Ada and Tzilla! The world was established for the purpose of procreation!*

Lemech's wives retorted, *Cure your own sickness first, doctor, before giving us instructions. You have been separate from Eve for a hundred and thirty years, and you tell us what to do?*

Adam took their words to heart. [He reunited] with Eve and a son was born. This son resembled Adam. Just as Adam had been born circumcised, [so was his son Shet] born circumcised. Eve named him [*Shet*]: explaining (Genesis 4:25), *For God Has Appointed me another seed instead of Hevel, whom Cain slew.* The name [Shet] also denotes *"founder of the world,"* since [Shet] became Adam's successor. Adam transmitted to [Shet] the [Seven] Commands which the Lord Had Revealed to him. [Adam] handed over to [Shet] the Heavenly Garments which the Lord Had Made for him [and] Eve.

The birth of Shet began a new Spiritual line from Adam and Eve. All of us, the Children of Israel and the Children of Noah are from this Spiritual line. This line from Adam and Eve is the righteous Line of Shet. There are many Spiritual people in this line...

The Torah Teaches us to overcome our anger. One should turn away from anger when procreating. It is better for one to be in a calm frame of mind when one procreates.

The Torah also Tells us that one can overcome their struggles, Genesis 4.7. One can improve. The Torah places the emphasis on turning from sin and on improving.

Gematria And Mysticism In Genesis

Genesis Chapter 5
Adam and Eve Are Equal

Genesis 5.1

זֶה סֵפֶר תּוֹלְדֹת אָדָם בְּיוֹם בְּרֹא אֱלֹהִים
אָדָם בִּדְמוּת אֱלֹהִים עָשָׂה אֹתוֹ :

This is the Book of Generations of Adam [singular] in the day God Created [singular] **Adam** [singular]. With [Spiritual] likeness, God made them [plural].

Genesis 5.2

זָכָר וּנְקֵבָה בְּרָאָם וַיְבָרֶךְ אֹתָם וַיִּקְרָא
אֶת־שְׁמָם אָדָם בְּיוֹם הִבָּרְאָם :

Male and Female He Created [plural] and Blessed them [plural] and He Called everything from Aleph to Tav of their name [plural] Adam [singular] in the day they were Created [plural].

Gematria And Mysticism In Genesis

Adam and Eve were created in one physical body, then separated later the same day. They were Created in the Lord God's Spiritual Image as were the Angels. God does not have a physical body. Pharaoh defined this when he said in regards to Joseph, *And Pharaoh said to his servants, Can we find such a one as this is, a man in whom the Spirit of God is?* Genesis 41.38

The writer John said,
God is a Spirit and they that worship him must worship him in Spirit and in truth, John 4:24.

Genesis 1.26

וַיֹּאמֶר אֱלֹהִים נַעֲשֶׂה אָדָם בְּצַלְמֵנוּ כִּדְמוּתֵנוּ וְיִרְדּוּ בִדְגַת הַיָּם וּבְעוֹף הַשָּׁמַיִם וּבַבְּהֵמָה וּבְכָל־הָאָרֶץ וּבְכָל־הָרֶמֶשׂ הָרֹמֵשׂ עַל־הָאָר׃

And He Said [singular] God [plural] Let us Make Adam in our image [plural] in our likeness [plural] and let them rule [plural] fish in the waters and birds in the heavens and with all animals in the earth and with all creeping on the earth.

Gematria And Mysticism In Genesis

Who was God Speaking with? The Sages say the Angels.

Genesis 1.27

וַיִּבְרָא אֱלֹהִים ׀ אֶת־הָאָדָם
בְּצַלְמוֹ בְּצֶלֶם אֱלֹהִים בָּרָא
אֹתוֹ זָכָר וּנְקֵבָה בָּרָא אֹתָם :

And He [singular], God [plural] Created [singular] everything from the Letter Aleph to the Letter Tav of Ha Adam / the man [singular] in His Form [singular] in His Form [singular] God [plural] Created [singular] them [plural] male / masculine and female / feminine He Created [singular] them [plural].

Here we Observe that God Created [singular]. They did not create anything.

Genesis 2.27

וַיִּיצֶר יְהֹוָה אֱלֹהִים אֶת־הָאָדָם
עָפָר מִן־הָאֲדָמָה וַיִּפַּח
בְּאַפָּיו נִשְׁמַת חַיִּים וַיְהִי

Gematria And Mysticism In Genesis

הָאָדָם לְנֶפֶשׁ חַיָּה׃

And He [singular] The Lord [singular] God [Plural - used as singular] Formed [singular] everything from Aleph to Tav of Ha Adam / Adam and Eve from dust of the ground and He [singular] blew into the nostrils the Soul of Life and it happened Ha Adam / The Man became a living Soul.

The Midrash Says, Adam's physical creation was twofold, male and female in one body. In front he was a man, but attached to him in back was a woman. Rabbi Moshe Weissman, The Midrash Says (Brooklyn, New York: Benei Yakov Publications 1980), p. 33

Right from the beginning God Created 'mankind' male and female, with equal Godliness and of equal worth. Neither was more in the likeness of God than the other, both were given the same Blessing by God, both together were given the name 'Adam'...*And He Called them Man on the day they were created* - i.e., He Called both of them Man - including Eve - because her formation was from the man, individually, however, she was called Eve (R. Meyuchas).

Harav David Cohen points out that male and female components were originally created in the single body of Adam (Eruvin 18a). Thus, when God Named him Adam, it was implicit that his female part - which was later to become a separate human being - was also called Adam, because male and female were two halves of one whole. Rabbi Meir Zlotowitz and Rabbi Nosson Scherman, The Artscroll Tanach Series - Bereishis Vol. I(a) (Brooklyn, New York: Mesorah Publications, Ltd. 3rd Impression, 1989), p 167

R' Yirmiyah ben Elazar Said... - The first man [Adam] had, i.e. he was created with two facial figures. The back was later separated to form the first woman, Eve... - As it states (Psalms 139.5) *[From the] back the front You Have Formed me.*

The Gemara cites a dispute concerning the appendage from which Eve was fashioned...
It is Written (Genesis 2.22): *Then the Lord, God, built the side that He Had Taken from the man into woman...* Rav Shmuel disputed the meaning of this verse... - One Said the side referred to was a

figure, i.e. man was created as a double figure, a male figure and a female figure joined back to back. The female figure was later removed to form Eve. Talmud - Eruvin 18a

(Genesis 5.2) *He Created them male and female,* which indicates that humans were created from the very first both male and female…

The Gemara Explains:
This verse can be explained as [taught by] R' Abahu… For R' Abahu contrasted the two Verses:

[1] *He Created them male and female,* referring to man's creation in the plural, indicating that both man and woman were created at the same time; but it is also written...

[2] *In the image of God He Created him,* referring to man's creation in the singular, [possibly] indicating that only man was created originally, not woman… [In actuality the one [Eve] was fashioned from the first [one Adam]].

Gematria And Mysticism In Genesis

Genesis 2.18

וַיֹּאמֶר יְהוָה אֱלֹהִים לֹא־טוֹב הֱיוֹת
הָאָדָם לְבַדּוֹ אֶעֱשֶׂה־לּוֹ עֵזֶר כְּנֶגְדּוֹ:

And the Lord God Said it is not good for Ha Adam [the man – which at that time included Adam and Eve] to be alone. I will fashion a help mate like [him] opposite [him].

Wife / Ee Shaw

אעשה

אשה

To Make to Fashion

עשה

אעשה

The Hebrew Letter ע Ayin Represents sight or insight… Our Creator Formed the wife with sight / insight.

The word Eeh Shaw meaning wife has the Letter Aleph א which may be exchanged for the Letter ע

Ayin. One must question the use of the word him when we know in fact it is them. Adam and Eve are in one shared body that is referred to as him in Genesis 5.1, 2.

We see that our Creator Endorses some separation of husband and wife. He Separated them. He Created them.

Originally Adam and Eve were one body and one soul. Then they were divided. They were separated. Up until this point we know they were in agreement or they could not function. However after they were separated they each had their own individual choices. The Word כְּנֶגְדּוֹ Cih Neg Doh means like him [but] opposite of him. This means Eve was opposite of him sexually. This also means that Adam was like Eve and that Eve was like Adam. She was created like him. HOWEVER if Adam would stray from the original Adam, i.e. the created Adam, then Eve would no longer be like the strayed Adam she would be opposite him.

Genesis 2.21

Gematria And Mysticism In Genesis

וַיַּפֵּל יְהוָה אֱלֹהִים ׀ תַּרְדֵּמָה עַל־הָאָדָם וַיִּישָׁן וַיִּקַּח אַחַת מִצַּלְעֹתָיו וַיִּסְגֹּר בָּשָׂר תַּחְתֶּנָּה:

The Lord God Caused a deep sleep to fall on Ha Adam, the man. [Both Adam and Eve were asleep. Both were not conscious.] the Lord God Took from the being... the double figure that was Ha Adam, [i.e. Adam and Eve] and closed the flesh in its place.

When our Creator Takes a woman from a man there is a wound left afterwards. The Torah Says that [He] closed over the flesh in its place. Anytime a couple separates there is a wound. The man has a wound and the woman has a wound. Make no mistake, there is a wound that requires closing. The time required for closing is different for each of us. The Word וַיִּסְגֹּר Vah Yee Sih Gohr means to lock, to close, to shut, to enclose, to bolt shut... When a relationship ends, when togetherness ends when sharing ends, when loving ends IT IS PAINFUL!! The flesh must be closed over.

This next part is AMAZING!! It is תַּחְתֶּנָּה Tah Chih Teh Nawh meaning to close over. However the translation does not explain what is at the core of closing over. The shoresh (root) of תַּחְתֶּנָּה Tah Chih Teh Nawh is חתן Chah Tawn meaning to wed. The point is that marriage heals the wound of what one has lost. So while one requires sometime to adjust after being separated from one's mate the real closing of separation comes with MARRIAGE of a new mate - not a relationship. A man needs a wife for balance. A woman needs a husband for balance. Together husband and wife possess the ability to be equal.

Genesis 2.22

וַיִּבֶן יְהֹוָה אֱלֹהִים ׀ אֶת־הַצֵּלָע אֲשֶׁר לָקַח מִן־הָאָדָם לְאִשָּׁה וַיְבִאֶהָ אֶל־הָאָדָם׃

And He, the Lord God, Built everything from the Letter Aleph to the Letter Tav from the side that He took from Ha Adam into [the most beautiful] wife and brought her to Adam [the man no longer the couple].

Our Creator who fashioned Eve built from everything from the Letter Aleph to the Letter Tav from the side that He took from Ha Adam. The result had to be the

Gematria And Mysticism In Genesis

best of the best. We notice from the Gematria of 68 for the Word וַיִּבֶן Vah Yee Vehn meaning, to build up. By building up the the material He took from Adam, our Creator provided חַיִּים Chah Yeem, meaning Life, and יָחֹן Yaw Choon, meaning Favor, Beauty, and חָכַם Chah Cahm, meaning Wisdom to Eve. This was not just for Eve's benefit. It was for all of our good. Our Creator Breathed Life into lifeless clay then our Creator fashioned life out of Adam's side.

וַיִּבֶן
Vah Yee Vehn
And He Built
68 = 50ן 2ב 10י 6ו

חַיִּים
Chah Yeem
Life
68= 60ם 10י 10י 8ח

יָחֹן
Yaw Choon
Favor Or Beauty
68 = 50ן 8ח 10י

Dear Ones, both Adam and Eve were created equal. Both were Created at the same time. Both Adam and Eve came from the same body. The body changed when the Lord God Took Eve from Adam. At the time of their separation Adam needed a wife and Eve needed a husband. Neither was equal any longer. Adam needed what Eve had and Eve needed what Adam had. Together they were equal. Separated, neither were equal! The flesh from where they were separated needed to be closed over and healed. This happened when Adam and Eve wed.

May each mate within marriage be sensitive to the other. May each mate seek out the advice of their mate. May each of us realize the great value and blessing of our mate!

The Talmud Comments *that [an individual] without [a spouse, a mate is not whole], for it is said, 'male and female he Created them... and Called their name Man' [i.e. only together, as man and wife, is [he / she] called Man],* Yevamos 63a.

May we each be Blessed by the Lord with joining in equality with our spouse and sharing the value of marriage, both those who are married and those searching for their spouse, Kah Naw Naw Hah Raw! May each of us learn and appreciate the great value our spouse brings to the marriage relationship.

Gematria And Mysticism In Genesis

Genesis Chapter 6
What's In A Name A Word?

Bereishis / Genesis 6.1

וַיְהִי כִּי־הֵחֵל הָאָדָם לָרֹב עַל־פְּנֵי הָאֲדָמָה וּבָנוֹת יֻלְּדוּ לָהֶם :

And it happened, when the Adam began to multiply on the face of the earth, and daughters were born to them...

Gematria And Mysticism In Genesis

Dear Ones the word that is normally used for men is אִישׁ Eesh. The word used here is הָאָדָם meaning, 'the Adam'. It is the fourth word from the right. We should ask why use the word 'the Adam'?

אִישׁ
Eesh
Man
א1 י10 שׁ300 = 311

הָאָדָם
Haw Aw Dawm
meaning, the Adam
ה5 א1 ד4 ם40 = 50

The difference between 311 and 50 is 261. This is why the title of this chapter is called, <u>What's In A Name A Word</u>? The difference between Eesh and the Man is הַדְּבָרִים Ha Dih Vah Reem meaning the words.

הַדְּבָרִים
Ha Dih Vah Reem
The Words
ה5 ד4 ב2 ר200 י10 ם40 =261

152

Gematria And Mysticism In Genesis

Both Eesh and [Ha] Adam begin with the Letter Aleph. The Letter ה Hey proceeding the Aleph is not part of the Word. The Letter Aleph in both Words is representative of our Creator. The Letters יש Yash mean substance, possessions, assets. The Letters דם represent blood. The world then spilt blood. As a result their blood would be spilt. They would die. They will not come back to life. They are gone. The eight survivors on the Ark however represent the Spiritual substance of the previous world. The eight survivors represent the the Spiritual Possessions handed down from Adam and Eve to Noah. The eight survivors brought the good assets of the previous world to the new world to begin again. The old physical world which appealed to the body was destroyed. The intent is for the survivors to have Spiritual desire and appeal.

Now for the next few pages we will recap a little of the history we have already covered. My intent is to provide a few more references and another Gematria.

When the Scripture Says, daughters were born to them this is in reference to the wicked line of Cain. This is the line born from Adam and Eve that took the sinful road. The Torah is Speaking of hundreds of years of breeding women children. There was a group of men that wanted women children.

Bereishis / Genesis 6.1

וַיִּרְאוּ בְנֵי־הָאֱלֹהִים אֶת־בְּנוֹת הָאָדָם כִּי טֹבֹת הֵנָּה וַיִּקְחוּ לָהֶם נָשִׁים מִכֹּל אֲשֶׁר בָּחָרוּ׃

2. And they saw, [who saw?] the sons of God saw everything from the Letter Aleph to the Letter Tav of the daughters of men, for they were pretty; [Good] Behold! And they took to themselves as wives from all that those whom they chose.

Commentators argue that the term for בְנֵי־הָאֱלֹהִים the sons of God is in reference to the 'sons of rulers'. We at B'nai Noach Torah Institute translate בְנֵי־הָאֱלֹהִים to mean Angels. The the occurrences where בְנֵי־הָאֱלֹהִים are written ALL MAKE reference to angels as being the sons of God.

Why are translators saying the sons of Rulers, i.e. Judges instead of God? The word אֱלֹהִים means

God and also means Judge or Judges who are considered Rulers, i.e. those that rule over the law. However in all other places where it is written בְּנֵי־הָאֱלֹהִים it is translated sons of God, meaning Angels. This is proper and this is how we translate בְּנֵי־הָאֱלֹהִים at B'nai Noach Torah Institute, LLC.

It is VERY IMPORTANT to grasp what Scripture is saying. אֶת־בְּנוֹת הָאָדָם כִּי טֹבֹת *'everything from Aleph to Tav of the daughters of men, for they were pretty'*. The Bible is Telling us that every woman on this earth was very pretty. Why? How? At this time women did not grow old as we know it. Women did not age. They kept their physical form... It was a great time to live because of the quality of health and vigor of women and of men.

When Scripture Says *'they took'* this is in reference to the two Fallen Angels, i.e. Uzza [Shamchazai] and Azael. Angels are Messengers of the Creator. They have no free will. They are required to deliver the exact message given by the Creator. In fact the messenger is so exact it often becomes difficult for the reader of the Bible to tell who is speaking, God or an Angel. This is the role God Created for Malachim / Angels.

In Genesis when the Lord was deploring the wickedness of man, two angels Shamchazai and Azael, arose before Him and argued, *Master of the Universe, didn't we tell you before the creation of man that he would be unworthy and should rather not be created?*

The Creator Responded to them, *If not for man, what purpose does the universe serve?*

They responded, *We, the angels, are sufficient reason for its existence,* was their reply.

The Creator Said, *I know that if you were to dwell on earth and possess evil impulses as men do, you would be even worse than they are!*

The Angels persisted, Just grant us permission to live among mortals and You will witness how we sanctify Your name!

Gematria And Mysticism In Genesis

Descend and do as you suggest, the Creator Told them. [They were given free will to live as humans]. Shamchazzi and Azael lived on earth as human beings. When they beheld the beauty of human women, they could not resist the temptation to sin with them. These [sinful] unions gave rise to giants of the generation before the flood. [Their descendants] committed the sins of murder, adultery, and robbery, [i.e. kidnapping etc.] Rabbi Moshe Weissman, The Midrash Says (Brooklyn, New York: Benei Yakov Publications 1980), pp 79, 80

These giants with superhuman strength had to derive power from some higher force just as Samson's awesome strength was a divine gift. To indicate the source of this strength the verse calls the giants b'nai Elohim, [בְּנֵי־הָאֱלֹהִים the sons of God], indicating that their strength and size was conferred by evil angels... Rabbi Meir Zlotowitz and Rabbi Nosson Scherman, The Artscroll Tanach Series - Bereishis Vol. I(a) (Brooklyn, New York: Mesorah Publications, Ltd. 3rd Impression, 1989), p 182

So when the Bible Says *'they took'* we are to understand they had the physical power to do as they chose. When The Torah Says whoever they chose this means they did not employ restraint. They used force to take whoever they wanted. This destroyed the entire social order.

They were fallen angels! They were supernatural beings. As supernatural beings they had sexual relations with humans. The result was giants. This improper and unholy mix of supernatural beings into the human race was certain destruction for all mankind had it not been eliminated from off the face of the earth.

3 And He, the Lord Said, My Spirit shall not always contend in man, shield him forever for he is flesh; his days shall be a hundred and twenty years.

וַיֹּאמֶר יְהֹוָה לֹא־יָדוֹן רוּחִי בָאָדָם לְעֹלָם בְּשַׁגַּם הוּא בָשָׂר וְהָיוּ יָמָיו מֵאָה וְעֶשְׂרִים שָׁנָה :

This is challenging. The term יָדוֹן meaning 'judge' or 'contend' or 'strive' speaks of the yetzer Tov, the good inclination within each of us. It seems that we are being informed that there is a place where man may no longer have a Yetzer Tov. In this chronological time frame before the flood when the forbidden mixtures of seed were occurring between angels, men and animals, the good inclination was almost gone.

Genesis 6.5

וַיַּרְא יְהֹוָה כִּי רַבָּה רָעַת **הָאָדָם** בָּאָרֶץ וְכָל־יֵצֶר
מַחְשְׁבֹת לִבּוֹ רַק רַע כָּל־הַיּוֹם:

And the Lord Saw for the wickedness of **man** *increased in the earth, and every product of his heart was only evil all the day.*

Again this verse points to the constant wickedness of man (Ha Adam) the physical man not Eesh the Spiritual man. So not all men were evil. There were a few good Spiritual men still in the world like Noah, Shem and Methuselah. The Spiritual people still possessed the good Inclination.

Notice the Word יָדוֹן meaning 'judge' or 'contend'

Gematria And Mysticism In Genesis

or 'strive' is the Gematria 70. Why is this significant? It was here that *the Lord Said, My Spirit shall not always* contend in man, *shield him forever for he is flesh;* his days shall be a hundred and twenty years.

Here man's [Ha Adam] days are being reduced. And again in Psalms 90.10 mans [Ha Adam's] days are reduced to 70 years the gematria of 'contend'. Now Moses, a spiritual man who wrote this lived 120 years. See Deuteronomy 31.21 Spiritual men often exceeded the years of the Ha Adam the physical man.

Abraham lived 175 years – Genesis 25.7
Isaac lived 180 years – Genesis 35.28
Jacob Lived 147 years Genesis 47.28
Joseph lived 110 years – Genesis 50.25
Levi lived 137 years – Exodus 6.16

Up until this time man [Ha Adam] had been allowed to live very long periods of time. Look at Chapter 5. Those that have my book, The Biblical Calendar, look at The History of Adam to Moses.

Gematria And Mysticism In Genesis

We are informed that Adam, Shet, Enosh, Keinan, Mahalaleil, Yered, Methushelach and Lamech died. If Cain and Chanoch were added to this group this was ten generations. What is the point? So few people from these generations had died. Human kind enjoyed many youthful years. They were young and energetic. During this time frame The Torah does not mention any sicknesses. No noted health issues. Everyone was a vegetarian. From the stand point of beauty The Torah is saying that great great great great great grandmothers were just as young and beautiful as their great great great great great great grandchildren...

Yet many from this generation will not be resurrected in the day of Messiah. God Said, When [in the resurrection] I restore My Spirit to the sheath... [בְּשַׁגָּם] [which is the protection for returning the souls to their bodies], I will not restore their Spirit [i.e. of this wicked generation] to their sheath, Lih Oh Lam, meaning to eternity. i.e. the world to come, Heaven, Garden of Eden.] לְעֹלָם בְּשַׁגָּם

4 *There were [The fallen] Nefilim in the earth in those days; and yes, also after that, when the sons of God came in to the daughters of men, and they bore children to them, the same, the mighty men from the past, with reputation.*

הַנְּפִלִים הָיוּ בָאָרֶץ בַּיָּמִים הָהֵם וְגַם אַחֲרֵי־כֵן אֲשֶׁר יָבֹאוּ בְּנֵי הָאֱלֹהִים אֶל־בְּנוֹת הָאָדָם וְיָלְדוּ לָהֶם הֵמָּה הַגִּבֹּרִים אֲשֶׁר מֵעוֹלָם אַנְשֵׁי הַשֵּׁם:

Over the years I have written many articles about the daughters of men and the fallen Angels... Purity, Fallen Angels, Sex and As In the Days of Noah.

The angels Created by God, came to earth and had physical relations with the daughters of men. This resulted in women producing giants called Nephilim, meaning *'the fallen'*? These Angels are identified as Uzzah and Azael.

Rabbi Zalman Sorotzkin comments, *The B'nei Elohim (6:2) and the Nephilim (6:4) are identical. ...From Nephilim were born the*

Gematria And Mysticism In Genesis

arrogant giants who rob and oppress and murder (Pirkei DeRabbi Eliezer Ch.22) *Now besides the base promiscuity that man had adopted, he saw just how far even the angels could sink. Here was a new wellspring of idolatry: Sexual liaison with the Nephilim and their descendants powerful men, murderers and thieves, who filled the earth with violence.*

There are many questions one should ask. Who are '*the same, the mighty men from the past, with reputation*'? One is certainly Cain he was very evil. There were other men of the same evilness that were transmigrated through the evil angels.

This is the second place in the first 6 Chapters of the Bible that makes reference to reincarnation of the soul.

Genesis 6.5,6

וַיַּרְא יְהֹוָה כִּי רַבָּה רָעַת הָאָדָם בָּאָרֶץ וְכָל־יֵצֶר מַחְשְׁבֹת לִבּוֹ רַק רַע כָּל־הַיּוֹם:

And He, God Saw great wickedness because of the

Adam in the earth, and every imagination of the thoughts of his heart was only evil all the day.

וַיִּנָּחֶם יְהֹוָה כִּי־עָשָׂה אֶת־הָאָדָם בָּאָרֶץ וַיִּתְעַצֵּב אֶל־לִבּוֹ ׃

And He, The Lord, Felt Sadness for Making everything from Aleph to Tav of Ha Adam in earth and He Grieved through his heart.

Some translators say The Lord repented for making man. This gives the impression the Creator sinned. One can do something perfectly good and later feel sad about what they did. This verse is about our Creator feeling very sad because humans chose the path of sin and would die for their choice.

וַיֹּאמֶר יְהֹוָה אֶמְחֶה אֶת־הָאָדָם אֲשֶׁר־בָּרָאתִי מֵעַל פְּנֵי הָאֲדָמָה מֵאָדָם עַד־בְּהֵמָה עַד־רֶמֶשׂ וְעַד־עוֹף הַשָּׁמָיִם כִּי נִחַמְתִּי כִּי עֲשִׂיתִם ׃

And He, the Lord Said, I will destroy everything from the Aleph to the Tav of Ha Adam whom I have created from the face of the earth; From Adam (man), to beast, to creeping things, and to birds of the air; for I regret for making them.

All flesh became corrupt. The Creator Took the best of what was left and placed them in the ark to preserve life on earth.

וְנֹחַ מָצָא חֵן בְּעֵינֵי יְהוָה :

And Noah found grace in the eyes of the Lord.

Noah who was a perfect man in his generation found grace in the eyes of the Lord. Even in the worst of situations this shows there is hope.

Gematria And Mysticism In Genesis

Genesis Chapter 7
God's Might as Seen in the Gematria 617

כִּי לְיָמִים עוֹד שִׁבְעָה אָנֹכִי מַמְטִיר עַל־הָאָרֶץ אַרְבָּעִים יוֹם וְאַרְבָּעִים לָיְלָה וּמָחִיתִי אֶת־כָּל־הַיְקוּם אֲשֶׁר עָשִׂיתִי מֵעַל פְּנֵי הָאֲדָמָה:

Genesis 7.1-3

And the Lord Said to Noah, Come you and all your house into the ark; for you have I seen you to be righteous before me in this generation. Of every clean beast you shall take to you seven pairs, the male and his female; and of beasts that are not clean one pair, the male and his female. Of birds also of the air by seven pairs, the male and the female; to keep seed alive upon the face of all the earth.

Genesis 7.4

For in another seven days I will cause it to rain upon the earth forty days and forty nights; and every living substance that I have made I Will destroy from off the face of the earth.

The Might of God is shown in this time of restraint. The mockers reveled. They carried on... They did not understand our Creator and the Angels in heaven had already begun to mourn their deaths. Noah and his wife, Na'amah and their children mourned the death of Methuselah who died 7 days before the flood. This was the end of the 120 year period. Then the Creator added another 7 days. Rabbi Avrohom Davis, <u>The Metsudah Chumash A New Linear Translation Bereishis</u> (Hoboken New Jersey, KTVA Publishing House, Inc., 1991) p 73

The Might of God is shown in the destruction of the world and the protection of those inside the Tava, the ark of safety. Thank God!

וַיַּעַשׂ נֹחַ כְּכֹל אֲשֶׁר־צִוָּהוּ יְהוָה׃

Genesis 7.5

Gematria And Mysticism In Genesis

And Noah did according to all that the Lord Commanded him.

כ 20 י 10   ל 30 י 10 מ 40 י 10 ם 40   ע 70 ו 6 ד 4   ש 300 ב 2 ע 70 ה 5 = 617

וַיֹּאמֶר אֱלֹהִים זֹאת אוֹת־**הַבְּרִית** אֲשֶׁר־
אֲנִי נֹתֵן בֵּינִי וּבֵינֵיכֶם וּבֵין כָּל־נֶפֶשׁ חַיָּה
אֲשֶׁר אִתְּכֶם לְדֹרֹת עוֹלָם:

Genesis 9.12
And God Said, This is the sign of the covenant which I Make between Me and you and every living creature that is with you, for everlasting generations....

הַבְּרִית
The Covenant
ה 5 ב 2 ר 200 י 10 ת 400 = 617

The Might of God is shown in the strength of His Covenant which has lasted over 4,100 years.

וַיֹּאמֶר מֹשֶׁה אֶל־הָעָם אַל־תִּירָאוּ כִּי

Gematria And Mysticism In Genesis

לְבַעֲבוּר נַסּוֹת אֶתְכֶם בָּא הָאֱלֹהִים וּבַעֲבוּר תִּהְיֶה **יִרְאָתוֹ** עַל־פְּנֵיכֶם לְבִלְתִּי תֶחֱטָאוּ׃

Exodus 20.17
And Moses said to the people, Fear not; for God has come to test you, and that His Fear may be before your faces, that you sin not.

יִרְאָתוֹ
His Fear
617 = 6 ו 400 ת 1 א 200 ר 10 י

Hebrews 11:7
By faith Noah, being warned of God of things not seen as of yet moved with fear, prepared an ark to save his household and in doing so through his actions he condemned the world...

We are to be in awe of our Creator's Great Might yet if we are obedient and follow His Commands as Noah did we will be fine!

Gematria And Mysticism In Genesis

גְּבוּרוֹת
God's Might
617 = 400ת ו6 200ר ו6 2ב 3ג

When a man and a woman come together to join under the chupah they are connecting. They are making a covenant. And wouldn't you know it, the marriage celebration is a week long. This is a time when the marriage is consummated and many blessings are said...

אִשָּׁה
Woman
306 = 5ה 300ש 1א

אִישׁ
Man
311 = 300ש 10י 1א
617 = 311 + 306

Dear Ones, we see God's Might in the relationship of a man and a woman and we see God's Might in the awesome fear we have for Him. And we see God's Might in Noah's obedience to Him. May we take these Gematrias and apply them in our lives.

Gematria And Mysticism In Genesis

Genesis Chapter 8
The Raven and The Dove

Genesis 8.1

וַיִּזְכֹּר אֱלֹהִים אֶת־נֹחַ וְאֵת כָּל־הַחַיָּה
וְאֶת־כָּל־הַבְּהֵמָה אֲשֶׁר אִתּוֹ בַּתֵּבָה
וַיַּעֲבֵר אֱלֹהִים רוּחַ עַל־הָאָרֶץ וַיָּשֹׁכּוּ
הַמָּיִם:

And He, God Remembered everything from Aleph to Tav of Noah and all the beasts and everything from Aleph to Tav of all the animals that were in the Ark. And He, God Caused His Spirit Breath to pass over the land and the waters abated.

Genesis 8.2

וַיִּסָּכְרוּ מַעְיְנֹת תְּהוֹם וַאֲרֻבֹּת הַשָּׁמָיִם
וַיִּכָּלֵא הַגֶּשֶׁם מִן־הַשָּׁמָיִם :

And the fountains from the abyss and the windows of the Heavens shut down and the rain from the Heavens closed down.

Genesis 8.3

וַיָּשֻׁבוּ הַמַּיִם מֵעַל הָאָרֶץ הָלוֹךְ וָשׁוֹב
וַיַּחְסְרוּ הַמַּיִם מִקְצֵה חֲמִשִּׁים
וּמְאַת יוֹם :

And the waters returned [to their places] from upon the earth continually and the waters returned and diminished at the end of one hundred fifty days.

Genesis 8.4

וַתָּנַח הַתֵּבָה בַּחֹדֶשׁ הַשְּׁבִיעִי בְּשִׁבְעָה־
עָשָׂר יוֹם לַחֹדֶשׁ עַל הָרֵי אֲרָרָט :

Gematria And Mysticism In Genesis

And the Ark settled in the seventh month in the seventeenth day of the month on Mount Ararat.

Genesis 8.5

וְהַמַּיִם הָיוּ הָלוֹךְ וְחָסוֹר עַד הַחֹדֶשׁ הָעֲשִׂירִי בָּעֲשִׂירִי בְּאֶחָד לַחֹדֶשׁ נִרְאוּ רָאשֵׁי הֶהָרִים:

And the waters continued to diminish until the tenth month, in the tenth [month] in [day] one of the month the mountain tops were visible.

Dear ones all these dates relating to Noah's flood are counted according to the Noachide Calendar which is according to the birthday of the world. If we were to calculate the flood in todays calendar the rain waters began on the 2nd month of the seventeenth day of the Biblical Calendar or on 11-14-2011 and ended on 04-12-2012.

When is the tenth month and first day on the Noachide Calendar? According to our present calendar it was 06-21-2012. Then forty days later on 07-30-2012 Noah opens the window of the ark and sends out a Raven. Seven days later on 08-06-2012 he sends the Dove. Then seven days later on 08-13-2012 he sends the Dove a second time. The Dove returns with an olive leaf. Seven days later on 08-20-2012 he sends the Dove for a third time. The Dove does not return.

Dear Ones, relationships while on the Tava were forbidden by the Creator. Rabbi Moshe Weissman, <u>The Midrash Says</u> (Brooklyn, New York: Benei Yakov Publications 1980), p. 97

And to make matter more strained the Raven was angry that the Lord prohibited the unclean birds from bringing seven pairs onto the ark while the clean birds like the Dove brought seven pairs onto the ark. As a result of his disgust and anger the Raven copulated while on the ark. This was an expression of his outrage. As a result the Raven was sent out of the ark because of his sin of copulation while on the ark.

We see the Raven's sin in the Gematria 277. The

Gematria And Mysticism In Genesis

Raven 277 Gave seed 277 and sinned 277 in the 277 night / evening with his help mate / helper.

הָעֹרֵב

Haw Oh Rayv
The Raven
ה5 ע70 ר200 ב2 = 277

זֶרַע

Zeh Rah
Seed
ז7 ר200 ע70 = 277

עֲבָרָה

Aw Vih Raw
Sin
ע70 ב2 ר200 ה5 = 277

הָעֶרֶב

Hah Eeh Rehv
The Evening
ה5 ע70 ר200 ב2 = 277

Gematria And Mysticism In Genesis

עֵזֶר

Aizer
Helper
ע 70 ז 7 ר 200 = 277

אֶת־הָעֹרֵב

Everything from Aleph to Tav of the Raven
א 1 ת 400   ה 5 ע 70 ר 200 ב 2 = 678

אֶת־הַיּוֹנָה

Everything from Aleph to Tav of the Dove
א 1 ת 400   ה 5 י 10 ו 6 נ 50 ה 5 = 477

When we examine the Words אֶת־הָעֹרֵב we should pay close attention to the last three letters of the second Word. These three Letters as they are arranged spell evening, i.e. ערב Erev. These three Letters as they are arranged also spell Aw Vahr, i.e. sin.

What does all this Gematria concerning the Raven mean? The Raven who is the most intelligent of the bird species, who is black, sinned at night by copulating.

Gematria And Mysticism In Genesis

הַיּוֹנָה

Ha Yoh Naw, [Jonah] meaning The Dove
76 = 5ה 50נ 6ו 10י 5ה

עֶבֶד

Eh Vehd, meaning Servant
76 = 4ד 2ב 70ע

מוּל

Mool / To Circumcise
76 = 30ל 6ו 40מ

לֵאלֹהֵי

Lay Loh Hay, meaning unto God
76 = 10י 5ה 30ל 1א 30ל

We see the pureness of the Dove in the Gematria 76. The Dove 76 was a servant and a helper who was set aside unto God. This speaks of Jonah whose name means Dove.

This is the difference between the Raven and the

Dove.

Next The Torah moves forward to Noah's Birthday, to year six hundred and one, month one, day one. The six hundredth year, in the first month in the first day is 09-17-2012. What day is this ? This is the birthday of the world. This is Rosh Hashanah.

This is as the The Torah Says, that the waters on the earth began to dry. This is the day Noah Removed the covering of the ark. Then in the second month on the 27th day our Creator Commanded 'Depart from the Ark...' This calculates to 11-12-2012 of this year. We have noted all these important dates in this year's Historical Chadashim (Calendar). God Willing we will be publishing these in this year's Calendar.

Each of these dates correspond to the Noachide Calendar. All the dates from Genesis 1.1 through Exodus 12.2 are based upon the Noachide Chadashim (Calendar). It is at this time that the Jewish nation is forged. The words בְּנֵי־יַעֲקֹב Sons of Yaakov / Jacob occur only 9 times in The Torah The last occurrence is Genesis 49.2.

The Words בְּנֵי־יִשְׂרָאֵל Sons of Israel six times in Genesis.

Genesis 14 is about Noachide battles, King Nimrod, King Og and Shem, Malki Tzedic, King of Jerusalem.

Genesis 16 is about Hagar and Yishmael who were Noachides.

Genesis 19 is about Lot and his family who were Noachides.

Genesis 25 is about Yishmael son of Avraham a Noachide.

Genesis 29 is about Lavan a Noachide.

Genesis 36 is about Eisov the son of Yaakov and grandson of Avraham. Eisov was a Noachide.

Genesis 38 is about Tamar the daughter of Shem and grand daughter of Noah who were Noachides.

Genesis 39 is about Potiphar and his wife who were Noachides.

Genesis 40 is about the Chief Butler and Chief Baker.

Genesis 41 is about Pharaoh King of Mitzraim (Egypt) who was a Noachide. Exodus 1 is about the new king in Mitzraim.

What is the point? The point is that Genesis is the Book of Noachides. The Jewish nation would not be formed until Exodus. The Jewish Calendar would not be formed until Exodus 12.2. That being written and said, ALL OF Genesis is for Noachides as well as the Children of Israel!! Dear Ones the first 2,448 years of History in The Torah is governed by the Noachide Chadashim / Calendar.

הַחֹדֶשׁ הַזֶּה לָכֶם רֹאשׁ חֳדָשִׁים רִאשׁוֹן
הוּא לָכֶם לְחָדְשֵׁי הַשָּׁנָה:

Exodus 12.2
The Lord Said, Today, This Month shall be to you [the Children of Israel] the head of months. It shall be first of month of the year to you [the Children of Israel].

From this point on all Scripture in The Torah is measured by Jewish Chadashim / Calendar instead of Noachide Chadashim.

It is at this point that Israel becomes a nation. It is at this point that Israel has a separate Calendar. The entire Sefer (Book) Genesis is a study book for Noachides. This is why each week we Discuss a Limood, one Chapter a week.

Gematria And Mysticism In Genesis

Genesis Chapter 9
Vegetarian Until 1657 From Creation then…

Jeff, a student at B'nai Noah Torah Institute, LLC wrote: I thought I understood the context of this Portion of Scripture but when I read it this time a part of Verse Five stood out. 'I Will demand an accounting from every animal' in regards to life's blood.' You can imagine the kinds of questions that one could entertain themselves with taking this portion out of context but that would not do anyone any good.

Dr. Akiva Gamliel any incite from you would help me understand this scripture in context would be greatly appreciated.

Jeff

Gematria And Mysticism In Genesis

Dear Ones, in this Chapter of The Torah humans transition from being vegetarian to meat eaters. Think of what this was like. For 1,657 years the relatives of the people on the Tava did not eat meat. Wow!

I want my steak well done please…
What is the point? Our Creator Required Noah and his descendants to remove blood from the meat that they would begin consuming. This is also a Command for the Children of Israel. How does one remove the blood from food?

First one does a proper kosher ritual killing. In brief this is what happens. A blessing is said over the kosher animal. The throat area where the veins come up the neck are severed with a very sharp razor under the chin. The animal bleeds. The heart of the animal continues to pump the blood until the majority of the blood is removed from the body. The animal is checked for broken bones, lesions on the lungs and any sign that would indicate sickness. Animals that are sick or injured are not kosher. Then the Children of Israel would remove a special vein, the sinew on the hip, Genesis 32.32. This is a Command for the Children of Israel only. Then the blood is drained. Salt is added to draw out more of the blood. The meat is washed. Then the meat is packed and sealed by a Mashgiach / a rabbinic Kashrut Inspector. Two seals are required.

Not any Mashgiach will do. The Mashgiach must be Shomer Shabbat for the Children of Israel, Shomer Mitzvot, i.e one who guards the Sabbath and one who guards the Commands of The Torah Given to the Children of Israel. The Mashgiach for B'nai Noach must be one who is Shomer Mitzvot of the Commands from The Torah Given to Bnai Noach. Genesis 9.1

Prior to this time neither animals, birds or fish were offered as a sacrifice or taken for food. That would be a sin.
Genesis 9.1

וַיְבָרֶךְ אֱלֹהִים אֶת־נֹחַ וְאֶת־בָּנָיו
וַיֹּאמֶר לָהֶם פְּרוּ וּרְבוּ וּמִלְאוּ אֶת־הָאָרֶץ:

And He God Blessed everything from Aleph to Tav of Noah and everything from Aleph to Tav of his sons, and He Said to them, Be fruitful, and multiply, and replenish everything from Aleph to Tav of the earth.

God as Judge Spoke to Noah and his sons. Why not the wives? The ladies are to cooperate with Gods Command to their husbands. Yet the men were Commanded so they could not say to their wives, God Said you have to have a relationship with me. Men are prohibited from Commanding their wives to have a physical relationship with them. A man must woo his wife. A man must earn his wives desire to mate.

Obviously reproduction is ONLY between a man and woman. Homosexuality is forbidden. The old world was full of bisexual, bestiality and rape... God Help us all please!! Relationships of men with men or women with women cannot produce children.

Being be fruitful, and multiply, and replenishing

the earth places much pressure on the man to attain a place of beauty with his mate. The man MUST do things his wife wants. The man must listen to his wife. The man must not pass off on the things his wife needs him to do to around the house, with the children etc. Other wise she will not feel loved and will not desire to have a relationship with him.

A man must be kind, caring, gentle and respectful of his wife. Otherwise she will not be willing to have a relationship with him, to bear his children to nourish his children and to help raise his children.

Noah and his sons were commanded to replenish the world. This also means to help restore all forms of life; plant, insect, animal, bird, reptiles etc. This means the earth needed replenishing.

Genesis 9.2

וּמוֹרַאֲכֶם וְחִתְּכֶם יִהְיֶה עַל כָּל־חַיַּת הָאָרֶץ וְעַל כָּל־עוֹף הַשָּׁמַיִם בְּכֹל אֲשֶׁר תִּרְמֹשׂ וּבְכָל־דְּגֵי הַיָּם בְּיֶדְכֶם נִתָּנוּ הָאֲדָמָה׃

Gematria And Mysticism In Genesis

And awe of each of you and dread of each of you shall be upon every beast of the earth, and upon every bird of the Heavens, in all that moves upon the ground, and in all fishes of the waters; in your hands they given.

Our Creator Gave to Noah and his sons all life in the Heavens on earth and in the waters. Man was awarded authority of all moving life.

Genesis 9.3

כָּל־רֶמֶשׂ אֲשֶׁר הוּא־חַי לָכֶם יִהְיֶה לְאָכְלָה כְּיֶרֶק עֵשֶׂב נָתַתִּי לָכֶם אֶת־כֹּל׃

Every moving thing that lives shall be food for you; like the green herb, I have given to you everything from Aleph to Tav of all.

Noah and his sons were permitted to eat all forms of life providing this was done properly.

Genesis 9.4

אַךְ־בָּשָׂר בְּנַפְשׁוֹ דָמוֹ לֹא תֹאכֵלוּ׃

Gematria And Mysticism In Genesis

However, flesh with its soul / life, with its blood, you shall not eat.

Kindness to all living things that have breath, that have a soul must be regarded. One cannot sever a body part from living beings. In essence the Torah is saying the blood must be removed from the flesh. The Blood must be separated. The blood must be removed. The blood must NOT be consumed. It is necessary for us to take the blood from the flesh.

Do Not Consume / Eat Blood

דָמוֹ לֹא תֹאכֵלוּ

Daw Moh – Loh – Toh Chay Loo

ד4 מ40 ו6   ל30 א1   ת400 א1 כ20 ל30 ו6 = 538

תֵחָלֵק

Tay Chaw Layk

To Take

ת400 ח8 ל30 ק100 = 538

לָקַחְתָּ

Loo Kaw Chih Taw

To Take

ל30 ק100 ח8 ת400 = 538

Genesis 9.5

וְאַךְ אֶת־דִּמְכֶם לְנַפְשֹׁתֵיכֶם אֶדְרֹשׁ מִיַּד כָּל־חַיָּה אֶדְרְשֶׁנּוּ וּמִיַּד הָאָדָם מִיַּד אִישׁ אָחִיו אֶדְרֹשׁ אֶת־נֶפֶשׁ הָאָדָם :

And However, everything from Aleph to Tav of each of your blood [which belongs to] of each of your souls I Will require; from the hand of every beast I will require it, and from the hand of the man; from man's brother I Will require everything from Aleph to Tav of the soul of the man.

This is a prohibition against murder and suicide. The probation extends to all forms of murdering or killing one's own self, God Help us Please. The exceptions are sanctification of the Lord's Name.

The Lord Says, I Will Demand an accounting for every drop of blood spilt.

This applies to killing for self justice, i.e. without a court ruling. This applies to accidental killing. God Requires accounting!!

Gematria And Mysticism In Genesis

Genesis 9.6

שֹׁפֵךְ דַּם הָאָדָם בָּאָדָם דָּמוֹ יִשָּׁפֵךְ
כִּי בְּצֶלֶם אֱלֹהִים עָשָׂה אֶת־הָאָדָם :

Whoever spills the blood of the man by man shall his blood be spilt for in the Spiritual image of God He made everything from Aleph to Tav of the man.

When man began killing animals it was necessary to establish that killing man was not acceptable. There is a proper way to take an animals life. There is a proper way to take even the human life of a criminal. There is an order to follow! There is a procedure to observe. The Torah is Instructing us in the sanctification of life. The Torah is Instructing us in the value of life.

The Torah does not prohibit humans from continuing to enjoy a vegetarian style of living. However after the flood the earth changed. It seems the changes may require a different diet for man.

Gematria And Mysticism In Genesis

Genesis Chapter 10
Speaking Through the Generations

Genesis 10.1

וְאֵלֶּה תּוֹלְדֹת בְּנֵי־נֹחַ שֵׁם חָם וָיָפֶת וַיִּוָּלְדוּ לָהֶם בָּנִים אַחַר הַמַּבּוּל:

Now these are the generations of the sons of Noah, Shem, Ham, and Japheth; and to them were sons born after the flood.

Gematria And Mysticism In Genesis

Dear Ones Rabbi Michael L. Munk writes in his book <u>The Wisdom in the Hebrew Alphabet</u> that the Letter ת Tav is the symbol of Truth and Perfection. We especially notice this in the Word תוֹלְדֹת Toh Lih Dot. Our World began with Truth and Perfection with Adam and Eve and our world will conclude with truth and perfection after our Messiah arrives. It's like this, children don't worry. Be calm because all that begins well ends well. It's true, even though along the way we humans get a bit distracted yet in the end all will turn out fine. Good will overcome all evil.

The center Letter of תוֹלְדֹת Toh Lih Dot is the Lamid. The Lamid represents learning. The Lamid represents teaching. The Lamid represents a life, a couple, a family, a congregation, a city, a state, a world with a purpose in it. That purpose is established and rooted in the Torah. The Teachings of the Torah have been passed along from Adam to Seth, to Enoch, to Noah, to Shem, to Abraham, to Isaac, to Jacob, to Joseph, to Moses and on to B'nai Yisroel.

תּוֹלְדֹת
Toh Lih Dot
Generations

Gematria And Mysticism In Genesis

840 = 400ת 4ד 30ל 6ו 400ת

דַּבֵּר אֶל־בְּנֵי יִשְׂרָאֵל

Dah Bayr - Ehl Bih Nay - Yees Raw Ayl
Speak to [the] children of Israel.
840 = 30ל 1א 200ר 300שׁ 10י   10י 50נ 2ב   30ל 1א   200ר 2ב 4ד

How were these Teachings passed along? Some teachings were written. Some Teachings were spoken. The Teachings that were spoken would be said. They would be spoken as in דַּבֵּר אֶל־בְּנֵי יִשְׂרָאֵל Dah Bayr - Ehl Bih Nay - Yees Raw Ayl meaning *Speak to [the] children of Israel.*

The world תּוֹלְדֹת {Toh Lih Dot} meaning 'generations' speaks to each of us. The Gematria is 840. The Torah Says, These are the generations of Noah, Shem, Ham and Japheth. How does the generations of Ham speak to us? How does the generations of Japheth speak to us? The fact is that The Torah for the most part follows the generations of Shem. It is the generations of Shem that speak to us. The generations of Ham and Japheth are mentioned here through Chapter 11. At the conclusion of Chapter 11 Avram and Sarai are introduced. So it is important to understand that The Torah for the most part covers the descendants of Shem. It is Shem that is the chosen.

Why then does The Torah Say these are the descendants / Generations of Noah if for the most part only the descendants of Shem are discussed? The Torah focuses on the hope for humankind. The Torah is clearly Saying the hope for humankind comes through the descendants of Shem.

It is to let us know The Torah includes everyone. We all are the descendants of Noah. We all enter through the same Tav of Toh Lih Dot. The Letter Tav represents Truth. Each soul comes from the original soul, Ha Adam. Each soul experiences the Tav, Truth. The Tav also represents perfection. We entered this world Perfect through Ha Adam Reshon and Chavah Reshonah {the first man and the first woman}. We will exit this world through the perfection of Mashiach.

Toh Li Doht it is like a house with both a front and rear door. That is to say one enters the front and passes through the back as from generation to generation... So even though we may become discouraged because we are not from Shem we are still part of the generations of Noah. One may feel let out because they are not the Kohan, a priest, yet we are B'nei Israel. ALL OF US came through the same door. We will all exit through the same door!

The Lord Spoke through the descendants of Shem. the Lord Spoke through B'nei Israel. We all benefit!

Gematria And Mysticism In Genesis

Gematria And Mysticism In Genesis

Glossary Index

Abraham - aka Avraham #85 and Avram - See Genesis 17.5 [Avraham ben Terach] - means *'Father of Nations'*.

Abram - aka Avram #87 - See Genesis 11.26

Abimelech - Avimelech #40 king of Gerar - means *'Father of king'*

Adam - aka [הָאָדָם] Ha Adam, Adam #120 Ha Reshon Adam #120 - meaning - *'man, the man, men, humankind'*.

Akeidah - The Akeidah עקדה - See Genesis 22 - See The Schottenstein Edition Siddur for Weekdays With An Interlinear Translation) - The Akeidah is a prayer in a Jewish Siddur which is prayed everyday. - means *'the binding, the self sacrifice'*

Aleph - [א] The Aleph #502 - #507 is the first letter of the Hebrew Aleph Bet / Hebrew Alpha Bet. The Aleph = One. The Aleph is representative of HaShem / the L-rd. The Aleph means - *'to learn, to train, one thousand'*.

Aleph Bet - means *'the Hebrew Alphabet'*.

Gematria And Mysticism In Genesis

Aleph to Tav - [א ת] When I use the words 'from Aleph to Tav,' I mean 'from the first Letter of the Aleph Bet, the Letter Aleph [א] to the last Letter of the Aleph Bet, the Letter Tav [ת].' The Eht represents being all inclusive from the beginning of one letter to the conclusion of another letter. *'The word Et is spelled Alef Tav, the first and last letters of the Hebrew alphabet. It therefore implies a transition from beginning to end. Rabbi Ishmael therefore states that its main purpose [in the instance he is referring to] is to indicate the transitive sense of the word "created."*

Rabbi Akiba, on the other hand replies that the very fact that Et contains the Alef Tav implies that it superimposes the entire alphabet between the subject verb and the predicated noun adding all things that pertain to that noun(Cf. Or Torah, Bereisheit). See <u>The Bahir</u> p p 108, 109

Amorah - Ha Torah Says, [עַל־סְדֹם וְעַל־עֲמֹרָה] 'On Sedom and on Amorah. <u>The KJV</u> says, *'upon Sodom and upon Go-morrah'*. However there is no [ג] Letter Gimmel which is the only Hebrew letter that has the 'G' sound.

Angel - See Malach - Angel #4397 means *'messenger.'*

Gematria And Mysticism In Genesis

Ark - Ark # 8392 means *'a box, a chest'*

Avram - See Abraham.

Avraham - See Abraham

Aveinu - [אבינו] means *'our father'*.

Babel - Bavel or Babylon #894. See Genesis 10.10; 11.9 - It was in Babylon where one language, Hebrew, was confused into seventy languages.

Bayit - Bayit #1004 means *'house'*.

Bereisheit - [בְּרֵאשִׁית] is the Hebrew name for Genesis. Bereisheit is the first word of Ha Torah. Bereisheit is the first book of Ha Torah. There are fifty chapters in Bereisheit. Bereisheit means *'in the beginning'*.

Bet - [ב] is the second letter of the Hebrew Aleph Bet. Bet #1004 - #1006 means *'house'*.

Bilhah - See Genesis 29.29 Bilhah #1090 means *'terror, disaster, calamity troubled'*.

B'nei Yisroel - [בְּנֵי־יִשְׂרָאֵל] - See Genesis 32.33 {He};

Gematria And Mysticism In Genesis

Genesis 32.32 Bnei Yisroel means *'children of Israel'*.

B'nai Noachides - B'nai Noach [בְּנֵי־נֹחַ] See Genesis 18.9 means *'the sons / children of Noach'*.

Brit Milah - [בְּרִית מִילָה] is the ritual circumcision. Brit #1285 [בְּרִית] means 'covenant'. Milah #4139 [מִילָה] means 'circumcision'.

Cain - aka Kayin [He]; Cain - Cain is the first son of Adam and Chavah / Eve. See Genesis 4.1

Canaan - Canaan #3667 [כְּנַעַן] is the land of Israel. Canaan means *'merchant, merchandise trader'*.

Chanoch - aka Enoch- Chanoch [He]; Enoch #2585 is the father of Methushelach [He]; Methuselah means *'education or training'*. However there is no Letter [א] Aleph or Letter [ע] Ayin which are the only Hebrew letters that have the 'Ee' sound.

Charan - is a city in northwestern Mesopotamia, just east of the Euphrates River. It is normally a seventeen day journey from Chevron. See <u>The Midrash Says</u> p 217.

Chavah - aka Chavah [He]; Eve #2332 - There is no Letter [א] Aleph or Letter [ע] Ayin which are the only

Hebrew letters that have the 'Ee' sound. Chavah means - *'life, living'*.

Chief Baker - *'officer over bakery'*.

Chief Butler *'officer over butlers'*.
Chief Executioner - [שַׂר הַטַּבָּחִים] *'officer over executions'*.

Chof [כ] is the eleventh Letter of the Aleph Bet. Chof means *'spoon'* or the *'palm'* of ones hand.

Commandment - [צוה] See Mitzvah Command, Commanded and Commandment #6680 come from the same root. Commandment is an 'order'.

Creator - Creator is a name I like to use for HaShem God, the L-rd God.

Deenah - Deenah [He] Dinah # 1783 is the first daughter of Yaakov and Leah. See Genesis 30.21 Deenah means *'judgment'*.
Divine - I use Divine to mean from or of God. Divine can mean holy as in the Holy Scriptures.

Dream - Dreams # 2472 recorded in Ha Torah are prophetic.

Egypt - aka [מִצְרַיִם] Mitzrim {He} Egypt #4714 . This is the country that gave birth to B'nei Yisroel. Mitzrim is at the northeastern part of Africa, next to Palestine. Mitzrim means *'heavy darkness, gloom'*.

Elifaz - [אלפז] is the son of Eisov and Grandson of Yitzchok and nephew of Yaakov.

Emeinu - [אמנו] means *'our mother'*.

Erev Shabbat - [ערב שבת] This is Yom Shi Shi / the sixth day in the evening, It is Friday evening.

Eisov - aka Eisov [He]; Esau # 6215 means *'hairy'*.

Eretz Canaan - [אֶרֶץ כְּנַעַן] aka Eretz Canaan [He]; the land of Canaan

Esav - See Eisov

Evier - aka Evier [He]; Eber #5677 is the great grandson of Shem ben Noach, the son of Noach. Shem and Eiver established a school / Yeshiva where Avraham, Yitzchok and Yaakov learned. Evier means *'to Hebraize, to [teach[the Jewish religion culture]'*.

Fo'c'sle - This is the extreme forward compartment of a ship.

Gematria And Mysticism In Genesis

Flood - When Ha Tenach speaks about a flood #3999 it is reference to the flood in Noach's time. The flood began in 1656 CF [from Creation]. See Dr. Akiva Gamliel's 16 month calendar.

Gabriel - This is in reference to the Malach / Angel Gabriel #1403 whose name means *'God of strength'* [He] or *'Man of God*. See Bava Metzia 86b - n (37)

Gematria - This is a systematic method of revealing and understanding Biblical exegesis through the relationship of Hebrew letters and numbers. Gematria applies to the Torah, Tenach, Prayer Siddurim and other such books. The origin is not Hebrew but possibly from Greek 'Geometria'
Gargantuan - Very large task.

Gematria Miluy - means *'each Letter of a Letter Hebrew Aleph Bet is spelled out.'*

Gomorrah - See Amorah
Ha Adam - See Ha Reshon - Adam #120

Hagar - Hagar #1904 was the daughter of Pharaoh, a Princess who was given to Sarah as a servant because of his miss deeds. Pharaoh tried to take Sarah for his wife when she was already married to Avraham. Hagar became the wife of Avraham. She bore Avraham a son, Yishmael.

Later Sarah told Avraham to *'Drive out this slave woman and her son...'* Genesis 21.10. Later after Sarah's death Avraham took Hagar back as his wife. Hagar's name was changed to Keturah. See the Artscroll Tanach Series, Bereisheit Vol 1 pp 965, 966

Ha Mikdosh - [בית מקדש קדוש] means the *'Holy Temple'*.

Ha Reshon - When one carefully examines Ha Torah they will notice that the original reference to [הָאָדָם] Ha Adam was to both Adam the first man and Chavah / Eve the first lady. See Genesis 1.27. They shared the same body known as Ha Adam. See Genesis 1.26, 27; Genesis 5.1, 2 *'This is the Book of Generations / Histories of humankind in the day God Created [singular] Adam [singular]. With male parts and female parts He created them [in one body]. He blessed them and named them [Adam]. on the day they were Created.'* See The Metsudah Chumash / Rashi p 54; See The Midrash Says p 33

Ha Reshon means *'the first man'*.

Ha Reshonah - means *'the first lady'*.

HaShem - Ha means *'the'* and Shem means *'Name'*.

Hevel - aka Hevel [He]; Abel #1893 was the brother that

was the first human being on earth to be murdered. Hevel was murdered by his brother Kayin. See Genesis 4.8. There is no Letter [א] Aleph or Letter [ע] Ayin in Hevel. These are the only Hebrew letters that have the 'Ah' sound. Hevel means *'emptiness, breath, steam'*.
Horticulture - is the art or practicing garden cultivation

Isaac - aka Yitzchok [He]; Isaac #3327   See Yitzchok Isaac means *'laughter'*.

Jordan River - aka [נהר הירדן] Nehar Ha Yarden is a river in southwest Asia that flows 251 kilometers / 156 miles and ending at the Dead Sea.

Judaism - observes the 613 mitzvot of ha Torah.

Kal Yisroel - means *'all of Israel'*.

Katan - means *'smaller'*.

Kayin - aka Kayin [He]; Cain - Kayin is the first son of Adam and Chavah / Eve. See Genesis 4.1

KJV - King James Authorized Version of the Bible 1611 .

Kohein - aka Kohen - A descendant of Aharon the Kohen Gadol / High Priest. The Kohein was responsible for performing duties in the Holy Temple.

Kohen Gadol - High Priest.   There is only one high priest at a time.

Levi - Levi #3878 is the third son of Yaakov and Leah. See Genesis 29.34

Lot - The nephew of Avraham. Lot #3876 means *'to wrap, to cover'*.

Malach - See Angel #4397 - Malach means *'messenger.'*

Malki Tzedek - means *'King of Righteousness'* is Shem the son of Noach. After the flood he was known as the king of peace and righteousness.

Mem - [מ] The Letter Mem is the thirteenth Letter of the Hebrew Aleph Bet. The Mem is used to define *'comparative thought'*.

Menasheh - aka Menasheh [He]; Manasseh #4519

Methushelach - aka Mesushelach [He]; Methuselah # 4968 [מתושלח] [מת] death [ו] and [שלח] to send - Methushelach means *'[when this child] dies send death'*.

Milkah - aka Milkah [He]; Milcah #4435 ; was the mother of Rivkah / Rebekah. Milkah means *'the queen'*.

Mishlei - [משלי] is the Book of Proverbs

Mispar Katan - is where ONLY the first number is counted. For examples: 10 is 1, 100 is 1, 90 is 9, 60 is 6 and 400 is 4.

Mitzvah - [צוה] Command, Commanded and Commandment #6680 come from the same root. Commandment is an 'order'.
Mitzvot - See Mitzvah - means *'Command'*.

Mitzraim - See Egypt

Mysticism - Jewish Mysticism is and integral part of the Chassidic movement within Judaism. The mystical school of thought known as Kabbalah. Mysticism explains many things not understood. Mysticism opens the door to esoteric thought.

Mystical - Mystical relates to mystics of Jewish though who study allegory and symbols transcending human understanding.

Mystically - See Mystical

Gematria And Mysticism In Genesis

Neshamah - [נשמה] Neshamah is the third level of the soul. Neshamah means 'Spirit Mind'. This is the intellect that permits us to connect with Creator. [רוח] Ruach is the second level of the soul. Ruach has mortal virtues and distinguishes between good and evil. [נפש] Nefesh the first level of the soul. The Nefesh is our animal like instincts and cravings.
[חיה] Chayyah is the soul that opens our awareness of the Divine life force. [יחידה] Yehidah is the fifth level of the soul that has the ability to unity with the Creator.
Noach - aka Noach [He], Noah #5146 - means *'rest'*.

Osnat - aka Osnat [He] Asenath # 621 is the daughter of Deenah who was assaulted by Shechem. She is the grand daughter of Yaakov and the daughter in law of Yaakov. As a child Osnat was driven from Yaakov's house by her uncles according to Pirkei d'Rabbi Eliezer. This was because her uncles were concerned that people would speak of licentiousness in their tents. They were concerned that people would think that they were morally perverse. Yaakov engraved a metal plate and put it around her neck. The words stated that whoever married her would be marrying a relative of Yaakov's family. Osnat was placed under a bush. A Malach took her to the house of Potifer in Mitzriam. His wife, Zulaicha raised her as their own daughter. Twenty-two years later Pharaoh ordered that Osnat marry

Gematria And Mysticism In Genesis

Yoseif. See Artscroll Bereisheit Vol 2 pp 1800, 1801.

Passuk - means *'verse'*.

Pharaoh - Pharaoh # 6547 means *'great house'*.
Pirkei d'Rabbi Eliezer - This is a Tannaitic midrashic book written by Rabbi Eliezer ben Hyrcanus.

Potiphar - aka Poti-phera, Potipherah #6319 was the step father in law of Yoseif. See Genesis 41.50

Potifer's Wife - See Zulaicha

Rachel - Rachel [He] Rachel #7354 means *'ewe, sheep'*.

Raphael - [רפאל]means *'Angel of healing'*. Bava Metzia 86b -n (360

Rashi - Simon ben Isaac, a French rabbinical scholar 1040 -1105.

Raw Shaw - means *'evil'*.

Reuvein - aka Reuvein [He], Reuben #7205 is the first son of Yaakov and Leah. See Genesis 29.32

Rivkah - aka Rivkah [He], Rebekah #7259 means *'team'*.

Rosh Hashanah - [ראש השנה] Rosh Hashanah is the birthday of the world. It is the day all created things stand in judgment before their Creator. Rosh Hashanah means *'head of the year'*.

Sabbath - [שבת] Sabbath [He] Sabbath #7676 is the seventh day of the week. B'nei Yisroel is commanded to rest on the seventh day. Sabbath mean *'to rest, to cease from labor'*.

Samech - [ס] The Letter Samech is the fifteenth Letter of the Hebrew Aleph Bet. Samech means *'support, i.e. One can be relied upon.'*

Sarah - aka Sarah or Sarai was the wife of Avraham. See Genesis 11.29 and Genesis 17.15. Sarah #8283 means *'a noble woman, a Minister'*.

Shechem - Shechem #7927 is a name for the prince of Shechem who assaulted Deenah, daughter of Yaakov. Shechem means *'back, shoulder'*.

School of Shem and Evier - See Evier

Sefer Ha Yonah - means *'The Book of Jonah'*.

Seven Commands - originate from Bereisheit 2.16. The Seven Commands were given to Adam and Chavah / Eve to observe.

Seven Laws - See Seven Commands

Seventy Languages - See Genesis 10.10; 11.9 - It was in Babylon where one language, Hebrew, was confused into seventy languages.

Shechinah - is the *'Presence of the Alm-ghty'*.

Shem - Shem #8035 was a son of Noach. Shem means *'name'*.

Shema Yisroel - [שְׁמַע יִשְׂרָאֵל] means *'Hear Oh Israel'*. See Deuteronomy 6.4 - 9

Shimon - aka Shimon [He], Simeon #8095 is the second son of Yaakov and Leah. See Genesis 29.33 Simeon means *'heard'*.

Shlomo Ha Melech - aka Shlomo Ha Melech [He], king Solomon #8010 *'Solomon'* means *'peace'*.

Spirituality is one who is a Spiritual person, i.e they observe the Seven Laws of the Bible.

Spiritualist / Noachide Covenant - This was given to Noach after the flood. See Genesis 9.8 - 17

Sodom - Sodom #5467 is the city that Avraham's nephew, Lot lived in that was destroyed by fire from heaven. See Genesis 19.24.

Taryag Mitzvot - [תריג מצות] are the 613 Commands from Ha Torah given to the B'nei Yisroel.

Tav - [ת] is the twenty second letter i.e the last letter of the Hebrew Aleph Bet. Tav means *'sign, mark'*.

Tehillim - [תהלים] Tehillim is the Hebrew word for the Book of Psalms. Tehillim means *'psalms'*.

Tenach - [תנ"ך] aka Tenach, Tanach or Tanakh is an acronym that identifies

[תורה נביאים כתובים] The acronym represents: the Writings [ך] the Prophets

[נ] the Torah [ת]. Christians refer to Ha Tenach as the Old Testament.

Gematria And Mysticism In Genesis

Terach - means *'imbecile'*.

Torah -[תורה] is Genesis {Bereisheit}, Exodus {Shemot}, Leviticus {Vayikra}, Numbers {Bamidbar} and Deuteronomy {Devarim} are the five Books of Ha Torah. The Five Books of Moshe {Moses} and the Pentateuch are other names for Ha Torah. The books of Ha Torah were given to Moshe on Har Sinai by God. In addition to the Torah, the Written Law, God Gave Moshe a more comprehensive explanation of the Written Law known as the Oral Law; both the Written and Oral Law constitute the Torah. Torah means *'Law'*.

Tzaddik - means *'righteous'*

Ur Kasdim - is defined by our sages as the fiery furnaces of Chaldee. See the Artscroll Tanach Series, Bereisheit Vol 1 348, 349; 515

Viceroy - One who rules on behalf of a sovereign.
Yaakov - aka Yaakov [He], Jacob #3290 is the son of Yitzchok and grandson of Avraham. See Genesis 25.26. Yaakov means *'grip his heel'*.

Yardon River - See Jordan River

Yay Tzehr Raw - means *'evil inclination'*.

Yay Tzehr Tov - means *'good inclination'*.

Yehudah - aka Yehudah [He], Judah #3063 is the fourth son of Yaakov and Leah. See Genesis 29.35 Yehudah means *'praise'*.

Yerushalayim - aka Yerushalayim [He], Jerusalem # 3389 means *'to teach peace'*.

Yishmael - aka Yishmael [He], Ishmael #3458 means *'He, God will hear'*.

Yitzchok - aka Yitzchok [He]; Isaac #3327 Yitzchok is the son of Avraham and Sarah and the father of Yaakov. See Yitzchok Isaac means *'laughter'*.

Yom Kippur - means *'day of atonement'*.

Yoseif - aka Yoseif [He], Joseph #3130 is the eleventh son of Yaakov and the first son of Rochel. See Genesis 30.25 Yoseif means *'HaShem added'*.

Yud - [י] The Letter Yud is the tenth Letter of the Hebrew Aleph Bet. Yud means *'a jot.'*

Zayin - [ז] The Letter Zayin is the seventh Letter of the Aleph Bet. Zayin means *'arms'* or *'weapon'*.

Gematria And Mysticism In Genesis

Zulaicha - Foster mother of Osnat. Wife of Potifer.

Gematria And Mysticism In Genesis

Torah References

Bereisheit Genesis		Bereisheit Genesis		Bereisheit Genesis	
Ref.	Page	Ref.	Page	Ref.	Page
1.26	91	2.22	67	4.1	60
1.26	138	2.22	141	4.1	114
1,27	83	2.22	146	4.7	135
1.28	41	2.24	63	4.25	134
1.27	139	2.24	66	5.1	137
1.28	64	2.25	99	5.1,2	144
1.29,30	58	2.27	139	5.2	137
1.31	127	3.1	80	5.2	142
2.6	86	3.1	98	6.1	151
2.7	83	3.1	99	6.1	154
2.10	86	3.2-7	96	6.2	162
2.15	84	3.3	131	6.4	118
2.16	39	3.5	81	6.4	162
2.16	41	3.6	81	6.5	107
2.18	93	3.6	82	6.5	159
2.18	143	3.7	58	6.5,6	163
2.19	44	3.7	84	6.13	107
2.19	98	3.9	44	6.17,18	120
2.19,20	90	3.17-19	87	6.18	119
2.21	144	3.23	116	7.1-3	167
2.22	66	3.24	116	7.4	168

Gematria And Mysticism In Genesis

Bereisheit Genesis		Bereisheit Genesis		Vayikra Leviticus	
Ref.	Page	Ref.	Page	Ref.	Page
7.5	168	25.7	160	10.1,2	25
8.1	173	32.32	187	22.32	45
8.3	174	35.28	160		
8.5	175	41.38	138		
9.1	64	47.28	160	Devarim Deuteronomy	
9.5	123	49.2	181		
9.1-7	121	50.17	53	31.21	160
9.1	187	50.25	160		
9.2	189				
9.3	76			Tehillim Psalms	
9.3	190	Shemot Exodus			
9.4	190			19.8	31
9.5	192	6.16	160	34.14	47
9.6	58	12.2	180	90,2,3	109
9.6	59	12.2	182	90.10	160
9.6	193	12.2	183	139.5	141
9.7	64	20	41	148.13	45
9.12	169	20.12	17	19.8	31
10.1	195	20.3	51	Mishlei Proverbs	
25.1	66	20.17	170		
25.1	67	34.6,7	110	8.22	108

ABOUT THE AUTHOR

Dr. Akiva Gamliel Belk

Our Sages Teach that one should run from Honor. I am a Ba'al Teshuvah, a Jew who has returned to Judaism. I am deeply grateful for those who supported Jewish outreach to assist Jews like me in returning to Torah Observance. I do not feel like a great man, but instead, a man who will stand before the Creator of everything in the universe and give account of my actions. My degrees will not stand before the Creator. I will stand before the Creator. I will be welcomed into His Presence not because I believe in Jesus but because: God Loves me and has forgiven every sin, even my blatant rebellious sins... because I acknowledge my sin before God and make a plan to turn away from that sin and make it right for my errors... because I try to Observe His Commands in the Torah. The Lord our God is gracious.

www.ingramcontent.com/pod-product-compliance
Lightning Source LLC
Chambersburg PA
CBHW060514100426
42743CB00009B/1313